Developing Performance-Based Assessments

GRADES 6–12

To my husband and best friend, Richard,
for all the thinking, talking, laughing, sharing, and caring

Developing
Performance-Based
Assessments

GRADES 6–12

Nancy P. Gallavan

CORWIN
PRESS
A SAGE Company

For information:

Corwin Press
A SAGE Company
2455 Teller Road
Thousand Oaks, California 91320
www.corwinpress.com

SAGE India Pvt. Ltd.
B 1/I 1 Mohan Cooperative
  Industrial Area
Mathura Road, New Delhi 110 044
India

SAGE Ltd.
1 Oliver's Yard
55 City Road
London EC1Y 1SP
United Kingdom

SAGE Asia-Pacific Pte. Ltd.
33 Pekin Street #02-01
Far East Square
Singapore 048763

Printed in the United States of America.

Library of Congress Cataloging-in-Publication Data

Gallavan, Nancy P.
Developing performance-based assessments, grades 6–12/Nancy P. Gallavan.
    p. cm.
Includes bibliographical references and index.
ISBN 978-1-4129-6980-2 (cloth)
ISBN 978-1-4129-6981-9 (pbk.)
    1. Educational tests and measurements—United States. 2. Competency-based educational tests—United States. 3. Middle school students—Rating of—United States. 4. High school students—Rating of—United States.
I. Title.

LB3051.G264 2009
371.27—dc22   2008037144

This book is printed on acid-free paper.

08   09   10   11   12   10 9 8 7 6 5 4 3 2 1

Acquisitions Editor:	Jessica Allan
Editorial Assistant:	Joanna Coelho
Production Editor:	Cassandra Margaret Seibel
Copy Editor:	Pam Suwinsky
Typesetter:	C&M Digitals (P) Ltd.
Proofreader:	Victoria Reed-Castro
Indexer:	Jean Casalegno
Cover Designer:	Tracy Miller
Graphic Designer:	Karine Hovsepian

Contents

Acknowledgments

The author would like to thank all of the colleagues, mentors, students, teachers, and the young learners who contributed their insights and inspiration to this text. Special appreciation is extended to Jessica Allan for her support of and guidance with this project. Nancy heartily thanks her husband Richard for his encouraging interest and continuous care, her colleagues Debbie, Terry, Tammy, and Gary for sharing ideas and opportunities, and especially the graduate students in the Master of Arts in Teaching program at University of Central Arkansas for the dynamic conversations about performance-based assessments.

Additionally, Corwin Press gratefully acknowledges the following peer reviewers for their editorial insight and guidance:

S. Michael Putman
Assistant Professor
Ball State University
Muncie, IN

Jennifer Sinsel
Eighth Grade Science Teacher
Marshall Middle School
Wichita, KS

Buck Wall
Department Chair-Social Studies
Hillcrest High School
Simpsonville, SC

Deborah S. Yost
Professor
Department of Education
La Salle University
Philadelphia, PA

About the Author

 **Nancy P. Gallavan** worked as an elementary and middle school teacher in the St. Vrain Valley and Cherry Creek School Districts of Colorado for 20 years while earning her master's degree from the University of Colorado and her PhD from the University of Denver. Prior to her current position, she was an associate professor of teacher education specializing in social studies and multicultural education at the University of Nevada, Las Vegas. Nancy has authored more than 60 publications including books, chapters, and articles in professional education journals, including *Secrets to Success for Elementary School Teachers* (2007) and *Secrets to Success for Social Studies Teachers* (2008) with Ellen Kottler and *What Principals Need to Know About Teaching Social Studies* (2003). She is active in the American Educational Research Association (AERA), the Association of Teacher Educators (ATE), the National Association for Multicultural Education (NAME), and the National Council for the Social Studies (NCSS).

Currently Nancy is professor of teacher education in the Master of Arts in Teaching (MAT) program at the University of Central Arkansas.

Introduction

The greatest joy of teaching occurs every time you realize that one of your students "gets it." The happiness will start deep down inside and then ooze out of you. You'll not only smile, you'll beam. At first, it may be hard for you to control your enthusiasm. Then your learners will see your satisfaction, sense your delight, and share in the excitement. Hopefully, all students who "get it" will recognize the moment it happens to them too. This scene illustrates your ultimate quest: to develop performance-based assessments and assessment systems through which learners know immediately for themselves when they understand the learning, have achieved the expectations, and genuinely "get it."

Once one learner "gets it," you will be inspired to ensure that all of your learners "get it" and as often as possible. These special moments capture what teaching is all about. "Getting it" inspires your learners to keep learning and for you to keep teaching. The secrets are to engage your learners actively in the learning process, to connect the learning meaningfully to their individual lives, and to check the learning frequently through different strategies that allow the learners to demonstrate anticipated outcomes in various ways, especially in ways that learners can assess themselves. Careful development of performance-based assessments also enables you to thoughtfully align the curriculum and instruction for your learners as individuals and as members of a shared learning community. As a result, you equip your learners for lifelong learning, preparing them for careers in fields that may not yet exist in an ever changing, interdependent, global society.

Effective learning and teaching do not just happen by accident. You may have been told that you are a natural teacher, and certainly some people seem more capable and comfortable as teachers. However, the best teachers have honed their knowledge, skills, and dispositions so learning and teaching become a finely tuned machine ready to transport everyone on their travels to their individual destinations.

Effective teachers are constantly seeking ways to make the whole process clearer and simpler for everyone so schooling is positive, productive, and practical.

For example, you can design the most elaborate curricular plans and prepare the most exciting instructional strategies. However, if you have not tailored your approaches to match your specific educational context and to fit your learners' needs and interests, unfortunately you may have wasted most of your efforts. Your learners may not make the necessary connections to the new ideas and complex skills you present; they will not be able to master their content standards and learning expectations. You will have to try again, and you may become rather discouraged. Your learners (along with their parents and your administrators) may wear out too. Maybe these results account for the high rate of burn-out attributing to the growing percent of attrition our nation is experiencing among our new as well as veteran teachers.

This text will reveal the secrets to success to help every educator who wants to create stimulating learning and teaching environments in their middle-level and secondary school classrooms for and with their learners. Whether you are a teacher candidate aspiring to start your career, a veteran teacher seeking more insights to improve your practices, a mentor teacher guiding a novice, a school administrator leading other educators, or even a teacher educator wanting to model appropriate assessments with your teacher candidates, this book will greatly improve your effectiveness and satisfaction before, during, and after the learning.

The ideas and examples awaiting you will guide you in developing performance-based assessments to strengthen your teaching, the learning, and the schooling in middle-level and secondary school classrooms. All three aspects happen at once. As you refine your expertise related to teaching, your learners will attend physically, mentally, emotionally, and socially leading to increased achievement of their learning proficiencies. When learning and teaching are synchronized, then the schooling is enhanced. The overall program fits together; rates of attendance, achievement, and completion increase. And everyone knows that improving your learners' achievement as shown on daily assignments, unit assessments, and standardized tests encompasses one of your major, if not the most important of all tasks. This text will guide and support you all the way.

Performance-based assessments allow you to plan your teaching and to facilitate learning experiences accompanied with engaging, challenging, and rewarding outcomes. In Chapter 1 you are introduced to the purposes for performance-based assessments, so you fully understand why you are doing what you are doing. And in Chapter 2 you explore the facets of understanding so you can plan your assessments to increase learner engagement and achievement.

Next you begin a three-part exploration into when to use performance-based assessments. In Chapter 3, you investigate the various roles of baseline assessments for gathering preassessment data by matching performance-based assessments with academic expectations by building on prior learning. In Chapters 4 and 5, you discover how to align assessments with curriculum and instruction and the many strategies for using formative assessments. In Chapter 6, you extend the conversation for administering summative assessments.

In Chapter 7, you analyze the five types of inquiry of performance-based assessments so you understand what information you are going to assess of your students. When you assess your students' learning, you are seeking all kinds of evidence so you can give them insightful feedback. In Chapter 8, you identify the five forms of appraisal that your students need to demonstrate learning across the curriculum. You want to use the most authentic form of assessment to showcase your learners' strengths and equip them to overcome their weaknesses. Then in Chapter 9, you combine the five types of information with the five forms of appraisal into a graphic organizer called a template to guide your preparation and practices. As one teacher shared with me, "The assessment template is the best tool I have learned in this whole teaching program. Thank you for making assessments so easy for me and my learners." Many examples are provided for you.

In Chapter 9, you also learn how to build and use rubrics. Again, a simple technique has been developed for you to incorporate rubrics into your planning procedures and teaching repertoire. Additionally, you are guided through the processes of creating rubrics with your learners. In Chapter 10, the many different approaches to assessment are connected with various kinds of evaluation for accountability. You may think the words *assessment* and *evaluation* are synonymous; however, they play extremely different roles that will assist you with your methods of accountability.

Each chapter includes special features. Planning and implementing performance-based assessments requires several interconnected steps. This text guides you in the beginning; then you will be supported in creating a system and making modifications to fit your own situation. Checklists have been included for you to follow the process quickly and easily. The checklists can be used for each individual learning experience and each unit of learning. You might want to copy these pages so you can follow the steps closely as you align your assessments.

Developing performance-based assessments can pose a challenging topic for many classroom teachers. Therefore, to extend the concepts and practices captured in each chapter, frequently asked questions with answers have been included. The questions come from teachers just like you. This text reflects your concerns and connects with your needs.

Each chapter also features graphic organizers to help you associate the vocabulary in a professional context. Diagrams are used throughout the text so you can visualize the processes. Finally, at the conclusion of each chapter, five activities have been written for you to apply the concepts and practices into your own teaching. When you discover the five types of information and five forms of appraisal in Chapters 7 and 8, you will realize that the activities parallel the approaches that are presented in this text. The activities will allow you to experience performance-based assessment immediately. At the end of the book is a list of readings and references that you may find useful.

On the Corwin Press Web site (www.corwinpress.com/gallavan612), there are four appendices. Appendix A presents the Standards For Teacher Competence in Educational Assessment of Students developed by members of the American Federation of Teachers, the National Council on Measurement in Education, the National Education Association in 1990.

Appendix B describes the four domains of learning, so you can be sure you are teaching holistically; it also itemizes the taxonomies and multiple intelligences to guide you in your instruction and inquiries. In Appendix C, you will find a poem written about performance-based assessments. I hope you enjoy and appreciate it too.

Appendix D offers a list of Web sites related to performance-based assessments, including the content standard Web sites, that many teachers have found to be helpful. These resources will save you time, money, and energy once you become acquainted with their services. Performance-based assessments encompass an area of study that many of you will want to pursue through graduate studies or professional development.

The hope is to share a zeal for performance-based assessments. Developing performance-based assessments can be a bit overwhelming with everything effective learning and teaching entail. Here's the greatest secret: this text is here to help you to become the best teacher possible so you and your middle-level and secondary school learners will shine with pride in your accomplishments. Let performance-based assessments be your friends!

1

Examining the Many Purposes of Assessment

How can I be sure that my students learn what I am teaching and what they are supposed to be learning? How can I involve students in their own growth and understanding? What kinds of tests should I be giving? How do I construct a test? How often should I give tests? What if my students do not do well? What if I don't like giving tests? Do I have other choices? And what do my comments on daily work and tests actually mean to my students? What do my assessments tell me about my teaching?

Do these questions sound familiar to you? Inquiries like these questions challenge most teachers, and like them, you may not feel adequately prepared to assess your learners. You tend to spend most of your time reviewing your content, perfecting your teaching strategies, and collecting resource materials. Then, as you get ready to put it all into action, you realize that your assessments need attention.

As a middle-level and/or secondary school teacher, you want to develop the most valuable activities and successful assignments so your students actively engage in the learning, easily connect new learning to their personal lives, and eagerly generate appropriate evidence showing that they truly understand or "get it." Your mission is to check their learning using appropriate performance-based assessments that are purposeful for you and your learners.

Demystify Performance-Based Assessments

Before delving into when, what, and how to assess to answer the questions posed at the start of this chapter, let's look at 12 general concepts related to assessment that establish a firm foundation. Teachers spend 30 percent to 40 percent, maybe as much as 90 percent of their time preparing, administering, analyzing, intervening, documenting, and reporting assessments (Campbell & Evans, 2000), so understanding performance-based assessments is critical.

However, experience reveals that many classroom teachers have found both the conversations and the processes related to developing performance-based assessments to be complicated and perplexing. Therefore, some teachers tend to avoid using performance-based assessments, while other teachers have adopted some misconceptions about performance-based assessments. It is important for us to demystify and clarify these ideas early in this text, so that developing performance-based assessments will be easy for you.

Define Performance-Based Assessments

1. *Assessment means much more than just a test.* Every time you check to see if your learners understand or "get it," you are conducting an assessment. You assess when you observe activities, listen to discussions, read written responses, view drawn illustrations, watch performances, and pay attention to body language. You assess before the learning, during the learning, and after the learning; you assess formally and informally, directly and indirectly, by choice and by chance. You spend most of your teaching time assessing your learners. This text describes many different practices, and the suggestions guide you in using performance-based assessments to improve the learning and, consequently, to enhance the teaching and the schooling.

2. *Almost all assessments are performance-based assessments.* You may have come to believe that only when learners are demonstrating outcomes such as reading aloud, calculating a math problem, conducting a science experiment, giving a speech, or turning a cartwheel that they are involved in performance-based assessments. Asking

learners to respond to a discussion question, to complete a worksheet, or to take a written test are other viable forms of performance-based assessments that you use frequently. After all, the learners are performing by demonstrating outcomes through speaking and writing.

3. *Assessment involves the learning, the teaching, and the schooling.* During assessment, you are collecting all sorts of feedback and data describing the effectiveness of everyone involved in the classroom. Learning cannot happen effectively unless teaching and schooling are working effectively too. Assessments do not pertain solely to your classroom and your learners' achievements. When you visualize your classroom, it is essential that you always view assessments holistically within a specific context occurring before, during, and after instruction; happening in your classroom, extending throughout the school, and connecting with the entire community; as viewed by the learners, the learners' families, the teacher, the school administrators, the school community, and the state.

4. *Assessment drives learning, teaching, and schooling.* As you develop your curriculum and design your instruction, you should be asking yourself four vital questions:

    a. What do my learners need and want to *know?*

    b. How should and could my learners *show* what they know?

    c. What should and could my learners *do* and when?

    d. Where will the assessments and feedback tell me to *go* (with my curricular design, instructional practices, resource materials, learning community, individual needs, program organization, and professional development)?

The four key words are *know, show, do,* and *go.* In the planning process, you decide what to teach, how to teach it, when to teach it, and so forth; you also must decide how your students will demonstrate or could show you what they have learned all along the way. And from each assessment, you must decide where to go next.

As you teach, ask yourself: *Did I cover everything? Did I include enough depth, breadth, and connections? Were my directions clear? Do the students understand the reasons for learning? Do I need to reteach any of the curriculum? Do I need to repeat, revise, or rearrange any of the instruction? Are the learners ready to integrate and apply their accomplishments in new and different ways?* You cannot make your next moves without deliberately collecting evidence and carefully analyzing where you are now, before you begin. It is essential that you view assessments holistically, as a shared process with ongoing reflection, inspection, and communication; assessments are not just an end to your learning experience (aka, lesson plans) or unit of learning.

Involve Learning Options and Opportunities

5. *Assessments need to be appropriate and authentic.* When you are checking the learning, you want to use a practice of assessment that best fits the specific learning situation. For example, if you want to elicit authentic feedback about your learners' spelling abilities, you could give a traditional spelling test listing words in isolation, you could ask your learners to incorporate the words into a description or story that features the words, or you could integrate the words into various parts of the curricular content so your learners use the words in reading, writing, speaking, and listening. The last two suggested practices are the most appropriate and authentic, as they are realistic for learning the words and using them in context to be remembered for future learning and applied for life.

6. *Learners should be given (and should help develop) alternative assessments.* Too often the word *alternative* conveys learning situations with less academic rigor or reduced scholarly expectations developed for learners who have been identified as unable to succeed in the "regular" classroom. In performance-based assessments, *alternative* merely means different ways or other choices and options. Perhaps the assessment would be unique or unusual, but alternative assessments do not entail or require unconventional or scary methods. The ideas offered throughout this text explore how to develop alternative assessments for and with your learners that are appropriate and authentic. When you include your learners, they will be quite impressed and resonate once you give them voice, choice, and a sense of ownership or agency (Bandura, 1989). Giving learners voice, choice, and ownership will greatly increase student attendance, engagement, achievement, and completion.

Incorporate Teaching Principles and Practices

7. *Assessments must include salience—that is, assessments must be important and relevant.* The forms of appraisal that you are using and the types of information that you are seeking should match the learning and learners, the teaching and teacher, and the curriculum and context. You want to develop assessments that you can describe as the best investment of everyone's time and energy. Try to avoid conducting assessments just to gather and record data because you presume you should. Your students (and their families) need to know why, when, how, and on what learners will be assessed *before* you begin the

instruction. Your forms of appraisal must be germane to the content and processes; the outcomes must be significant for the learning to be recognized now, integrated later, and used throughout life.

8. *Assessments must include validity—that is, assessments must be suitable and applicable.* Again, it is all about a justified fit. You must be able to defend how the selected form of appraisal will elicit a particular type of information. At some point, a learner, parent, colleague, and/or administrator will ask you to explain your choices based on legitimate purposes and detailed procedures. And you want to be sure your learners can demonstrate proficiency with the content and processes in ways that are developmentally appropriate and rightfully showcase their accomplishments and achievements.

9. *Assessments must include reliability—that is, assessments must be dependable and consistent.* To be reliable means you can count on the assessment every time you use it to give constant results. You want to be able to explain the significance or why this assessment is the most effective and efficient. Once you begin teaching, most likely you will create a group of 5 to 10 forms of appraisal probing 5 to 10 types of information that you will use nearly every time you assess your learners. Your learners (and their families) will appreciate consistency in your practices of assessment, and you can refine and expand your routine with time and experience.

10. *Assessments must include fidelity—that is, assessments must be understandable and objective.* Fidelity ensures the purpose(s) of your assessments. Your assessments must be planned, prepared, and conducted so that you and your learners clearly comprehend what is being assessed, how it will be assessed, and why it is being assessed. In order for your assessments to be effective, you must attend to the clarity and fairness of your communications in the directions and questions on the assessments followed by the feedback and scoring after the assessments.

11. *Assessments must include robustness—that is, assessments must be deliberate and mindful of depth, breadth, and opportunity.* Assessments should be long enough to cover the subject yet short enough to be interesting. Learners must be allowed to provide adequate evidence of their learning with assorted ways of expressing their knowledge, skills, and dispositions. You want your assessments to serve as the capstone to the immediate learning and to provide the connection to the next adventure.

12. *Assessment must include expectations.* You need to determine through narrative description, checklist, percentage, and so forth the levels of proficiency that are satisfactory and unsatisfactory for each

assessment. You have to decide in advance of the assessment, scoring, and feedback if and how learners will have demonstrated mastery of each objective.

Assessments are easy to understand and to apply in both concept and practice. By aligning your curriculum and instruction with the assessment, you will find that the learning, your teaching, and the schooling will make much more sense to your students, their families, you, and your administrators. Now your assessments are positive, productive, and practical. What more could you want? Plus, your classroom will become more alive and engaging; and you will enjoy your work much more.

Table 1.1 recaps the 12 concepts about performance-based assessments. As a quick preassessment to check your entry-level awareness

Table 1.1   12 Basic Concepts About Performance-Based Assessments

1. Assessment means much more than just a test.

2. Almost all assessments are performance-based assessments.

3. Assessment involves the learning, the teaching, *and* the schooling.

4. Assessment drives the learning, teaching, and schooling.

5. Assessments need to be appropriate and authentic.

6. Learners should be given (and should help develop) alternative assessments to ensure learner voice, choice, and ownership (agency).

7. Assessments must include salience—that is, they are important and relevant. Salience relates to the description: What assessments match the content and processes?

8. Assessments must include validity—that is, they are suitable and applicable. Validity relates to the justification: How do these assessments showcase the learners and learning?

9. Assessments must include reliability—that is, they are dependable and consistent. Reliability relates the significance: Why are these assessments effective for the teacher and teaching?

10. Assessments must include fidelity—that is, they are understandable and objective. Fidelity relates to the purpose: Do these assessments communicate clearly and fairly?

11. Assessments must include robustness—that is, they are deliberate and mindful of depth, breadth, and opportunity. Robustness relates to richness: Do these assessments allow learners to provide adequate evidence of their learning.

12. Assessments must include expectations that are prepared in advance to determine multiple levels of proficiency for each objective.

about assessments, examine your thinking related to each concept. Do you agree? How do you incorporate these concepts into your practices?

Understand the Six Components of Assessment

Since performance-based assessments drive the learning, the teaching, and the schooling, they operate in a unified balanced that includes the following six interconnected components:

1. Each learner's individuality and background

2. Each learner's prior knowledge and experiences as part of the group of learners with constructed knowledge and shared experiences

3. The teacher's (*your*) expertise and expectations

4. The teacher's (*your)* organization and readiness

5. The curricular content and academic standards, and

6. The learning community context

These six components provide you with valuable information that unlock the secrets to your learners' achievement and your own success during your preassessments, formative assessments, and summative assessments. Figure 1.1 provides a frame for the overall assessment process.

Know Your Learners

In Assessment Component 1, you focus on each learner's individuality and background. You want to know all you can about your learners, both individually and as members of various groups. You want to familiarize yourself with their cultural backgrounds, personal interests, and learning styles. This component might seem like the most obvious one for teachers to understand. Ask yourself: *How can my students learn effectively and efficiently unless I know them as individual people?* However, too often teachers focus more on themselves and on the curricular content rather than on their learners as individuals, almost as if they were teaching in a vacuum.

For example, if you are teaching about nutrition, you want to discover the kinds of foods that your learners eat; the kinds of foods they like, dislike, and realize are good for them; foods they eat during

Figure 1.1   Six Components of Assessment

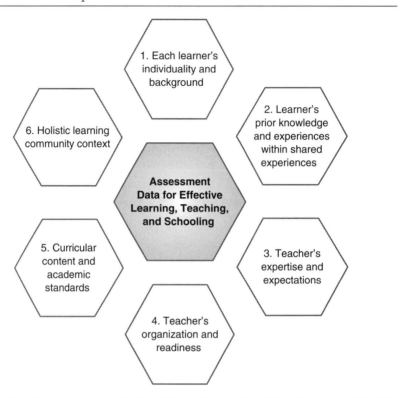

family celebrations; and the ways they prefer for investigating unknown foods, such as smelling, touching, and tasting different kinds of foods. Effective teachers become acquainted with their learners as unique people. You and your learners will enjoy delving into getting to know one another as individuals.

Assessment Component 1 works closely with Assessment Component 2. Now you focus on each learner's prior knowledge and experiences. You want to find out the content and processes each student has already learned and the various ways the students have either applied or connected the learning to prior learning in this content area, other content, and the world around each one of them. Getting to know your learners academically extends into the constructed knowledge and shared experiences that have occurred within prior classroom learning. Ask yourself: *How can my students learn effectively and efficiently unless I know them as individual learners?*

For example, if you are teaching your students about adjectives and adverbs, you want to explore and recognize the kinds of learners they are, that is, English language learners (ELL), gifted and talented learners (G/T), special education learners (SPED), and so forth. If the learners are new to you, you can read the students' cumulative files, talk with their former teachers, engage in conversations with the learners, and give them opportunities to produce and share brief writing samples.

Effective teachers tend to pursue all four of these assessment practices. Then, continuing our example, you want to investigate your learners' knowledge and experiences with adjectives and adverbs. This is the time to conduct a quick KWHL, asking the learners what they *Know,* what they *Wonder,* ways they will confirm *How* they learn, and what they would like to *Learn* next. You can preassess using the KWHL strategy as a formal or informal class conversation with or without writing. Organizing your preassessments is your choice and should fit your purposes.

Reflect on Your Practices

Some teachers spend disproportionately large amounts of time and energy on Assessment Components 3 and 4: the teachers' own expertise and expectations paired with the teachers' organization and readiness. Teachers tend to teach what they know, what they can do, and what they want to teach rather than focusing on the students as people with personal interests and learners with prior knowledge and experiences. Ask yourself: *How can my students learn effectively and efficiently if I am overly concerned with my own expertise and readiness?*

Likewise, many teachers place too much emphasis on Assessment Component 5: curricular content and academic standards. Responsibly, each teacher should refer to the student learning expectations guiding the state and school district. However, many teachers teach *to* the standards and assess the learning expectations almost exclusively of or away from the learners and their individual accomplishments. Regrettably, the learning may be taught in isolation and not integrated across the curriculum; the learning may not relate to the lives of the students and/or the real world. When these events occur, many students fail to retain the learning, apply it appropriately at a later time, or appreciate its contributions to our world. Ask yourself: *How can my students learn effectively and efficiently if I concentrate exclusively on the state standards?*

Assessment Component 6, the learning community context, emphasizes connections between and among the learners, the teaching, and the world—near and far; yesterday, today, and tomorrow. You will teach many different topics and issues that will be new and different to your learners (and perhaps new and different to you too).

In order for your students to use the vocabulary, understand the concepts, and apply the practices, you have to make meaningful connections and model the joy of learning.

That means that you place the learning experiences or units of learning within a learning community context. Your students will gain much more understanding and apply the learning much more quickly and authentically when you put the learning into an environment and situation enriched with multiple perspectives; then the learners can identify and apply to their own contemporary lives. Ask yourself: *How can my students learn effectively and efficiently unless I create an inviting, exciting, and igniting sense of place?* Unfortunately, many teachers overlook the value of a student-centered learning community context when assessing their learners.

Clarify Responsibilities for Learner Progress

The responsibilities for recording learner progress can be discussed using three different terms: *assessment, evaluation,* and *accountability.* Unfortunately, many educators use these three terms interchangeably, showing their newness and discomfort with performance-based assessments. While the concepts are closely related, each word serves a distinctly different responsibility necessary for recording learning progress and achievement. It is helpful to establish the definition of each word and to describe it thoroughly so you can discern and apply its individual meaning and usefulness.

Assessment: Collecting evidence for measuring understanding of and progress toward learning short-term or immediate objectives

Evaluation: Analyzing and deciding the degree to which learners have achieved understanding and have mastered proficiency of long-term outcomes toward learning goals

Accountability: Documenting results and communicating accomplishments; recording and reporting findings to others

Each responsibility for recording student progress fulfills unique tasks for measuring, determining, and reporting learners' outcomes and achievements. Yet the three responsibilities operate holistically, so it does not matter where you start your thinking about the three responsibilities. You may want to focus on the methods of accountability, then move to systems of evaluations, and return to your practices of assessments. As you concentrate on your practices of assessments, simultaneously you want to think about your systems of evaluations and methods of accountability. You cannot accomplish any of the three responsibilities without involving the other two responsibilities of learner achievement as reflected by your assessment practices, evaluation systems, and accountability methods. You can remember the three responsibilities as they are shown in Figure 1.2.

Figure 1.2 Three Responsibilities for Recording Learner Progress

A diamond represents your assessment practices; you strive for each of your learners to shine. Plus a diamond has four sides, noting the four stages of your assessment practices: (1) as you plan, (2) before the learning, (3) during the learning, and (4) after the learning. A triangle represents your evaluation systems. The purpose of assessment is to provide feedback relative to the three sides of the triangle: (1) the learners and learning, (2) the teacher and teaching, and (3) the learning experience and environment corresponding to the six components of assessment. A hexagon, the shape of a stop sign, represents your accountability methods. You are the final stop for maintaining documents and reporting progress to students, families, and administration.

Picture the Continuous Flow of Assessment

We now know that *assessment means collecting evidence of progress.* Assessment encompasses a continuous flow of practices that occur before, during, after, and long after the learning and teaching. Stakeholders include the teacher, the learners in the classroom, and everyone outside the classroom, such as families, administrators, community members, and so forth. Information or data gathered from assessments should inform the teacher about all six components of assessment.

Most teachers, learners, and parents think of assessments primarily as pencil-and-paper tests. However, written assessments certainly can be constructed in many different ways and definitely play important roles in assessment practices (O'Malley & Valdez Pierce, 1996). Some teachers think that performance-based assessments include only activities during which learners do something to demonstrate or show their achievement, such as giving a speech, writing a story, calculating a math problem, conducting a science experiment, or navigating a computer program. Sometimes performance-based assessments are called "alternative assessments," indicating that they are not the usual, normal, or frequently used assessments. Alternative assessments may be viewed as not being as important for evaluating final outcomes.

Therefore, there are three main points to keep in mind about assessments when you picture the continuous flow of assessment:

1. Nearly every assessment is a performance-based assessment (Stiggins, 2008).

2. Every kind of assessment practice is equally important and should be selected to accomplish complex and significant tasks, to apply to realistic situations, or to solve authentic problems (Herman, Aschbacher, & Winters, 1992).

3. Pencil-and-paper tasks, including tests, may qualify as performance-based assessments that should and must be used, albeit, judiciously (Airasian & Miranda, 2002).

Throughout this text, references to performance-based assessments include all varieties of evidence and feedback.

Start With Assessments and Objectives

You will spend most of your time as a teacher assessing in one of three ways: observing, listening, and reading. You are assessing *short-term outcomes* or *immediate objectives*. You can assess a single learning experience or several learning experiences collectively. The key to effective assessment is frequency; you want to assess often so you are sure your learners comprehend the immediate knowledge, skills, and dispositions necessary to continue the learning and make meaningful connections.

You will determine the objectives for each learning experience that you facilitate throughout the school day. Simultaneously you will be assessing academic as well as behavioral expectations. You will collect evidence, provide feedback, and record progress many times each day. Later chapters will equip you with a multitude of strategies to conduct formal and informal assessments as well as offer many cautions to consider throughout the process of assessment, evaluation, and accountability.

As you prepare to assess your learning objectives, it is essential to ensure that salience, validity, reliability, fidelity, and robustness are present in every assessment; think about the 12 basic concepts introduced in the first part of this chapter. Let's consider a learning experience when you are assessing your learners' progress in identifying the main ideas in a written passage. Check for

- *Salience.* Selected passages feature main ideas that are important for learners to know (remember . . . salience describes what).
- *Validity.* Identified main ideas have meaning for the learners and connect with prior learning (validity justifies how).
- *Reliability.* Identified main ideas give you the evidence you are seeking (reliability signifies why).
- *Fidelity.* Selected passages are readable and meaningful, directions are clear and achievable, feedback to learners is positive and productive (fidelity ensures comprehension and objectivity).
- *Robustness.* Assessment instrument includes an adequate number and variety of passages to demonstrate proficiency at multiple levels (robustness encompasses breadth, depth, and opportunity).
- *Expectations.* Descriptive checklists of expectations account for multiple levels of proficiency that may apply to the whole group or to individual learners.

Differentiate Assessment From Evaluation

After you have finished teaching a series of learning experiences, a whole unit of learning, or the entire course of study at the end of the quarter or school year, you conduct an evaluation by analyzing and deciding the degree to which learners have achieved understanding and have mastered proficiency of long-term outcomes toward learning goals.

As you design your curriculum and instruction, *you identify big ideas that you want your learners to take with them into the future.* Big ideas are called *goals.* For example, if you are teaching a unit of learning in math about long division, your objectives for your learners might be to calculate the quotients. You could assess your learners' progress toward fulfilling the objectives daily, as your objectives expand from simple division to more complex division problems.

Throughout the unit of learning, you assess your learners' progress frequently. Your assessments match the objectives or short-term outcomes. You could administer written tests with multiple choice, true/false, and calculations. You could ask your learners to show you the process, and/or you could conference with each learner, asking her or him to explain the process orally. Most likely, you will include a combination of assessments. Then you review all of the assessments collected throughout the unit, and you decide, that is, evaluate, if each of your learners fulfilled the goals for the unit.

The goals probably included knowing when or the most important times to divide, recognizing correct and incorrect quotients, completing the steps required to calculate the quotient, and applying the numbers in the quotient to answer the question in a word problem. If your learners have achieved all of the goals, then you can assign a letter grade on some type of report form. During the evaluation process, you review all of the formal and informal assessments that you have collected, and record the results (see Figure 1.3).

Figure 1.3   Relationship of Assessment, Evaluation, and Accountability

Goals for the Learning Experience (Lesson Plan) or Unit of Learning (Unit Plan)				
Objective #1	leads to	Assessment #1		
Objective #2	leads to	Assessment #2		
Objective #3	leads to	Assessment #3		
		Assessment Set #1	leads to	Evaluation #1
		Assessment Set #2	leads to	Evaluation #2
		Assessment Set #3	leads to	Evaluation #3
All Assessments and Evaluations			lead to	Accountability

Connect With Accountability

Throughout the assessment and evaluation processes, you record progress and report your findings in various ways. Evaluation is an analysis of an accumulation of many different assessments related to the same topic frequently taught over several weeks called a "unit of learning." Evaluations usually become the final grade in a course or the completion of requirements in a particular program or course of study. The purpose of evaluation is to provide feedback relative to the three sides of the triangle (refer back to Figure 1.2).

Once a unit of learning has ended, you need feedback about each of the learners and the learning experiences integral to the unit. You also need to know if you and your teaching were effective and efficient. Not all teachers connect with all learners and vice versa; you want to reflect on your patterns so you can make changes and improvements. Finally, you need feedback about the curriculum and content related to the learning experience, sequence of learning experiences, and the learning environment.

These events lead to accountability. *Accountability refers to documenting results and communicating accomplishments; recording and reporting findings with others.* You will communicate with learners, their families, your colleagues, and your administrators when necessary; plus you will document results in learners' records. There are many different ways to communicate results of both the assessments and evaluations: on the assessment items, daily or weekly progress report notes, checklists or rubrics, report forms, conferences, telephone calls, e-mail messages, and digital postings. Accountability is explored in greater depth in Chapter 10.

Expanding the graphic organizer on accountability (see Figure 1.4) helps you to make the connections between and among assessments, evaluations, and accountability. This text provides you with all of the vocabulary, concepts, and practices related to performance-based assessments to strengthen the learning, teaching, and schooling. However, you must identify and organize your assessment practices to meet the needs and interests of each learner and the setting. You are also responsible for your accountability to the learners, their families, the school, district, and state, documented in various systems of evaluation. None of your assessments, evaluations, or accountability records will make any sense if you do not consider your particular classroom of learners and the community context first.

Figure 1.4   Elements of Assessment, Evaluation, and Accountability

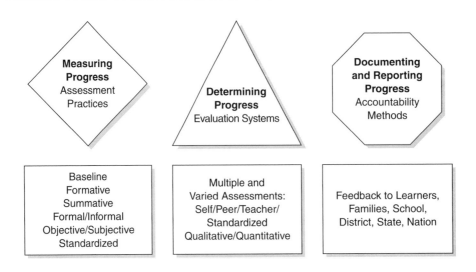

The good news is you can do it! And the guidelines in this text are here to help you. As you prepare for a particular grade level and all your subject areas, simultaneously you need to consider a variety of learning needs and interests. Most likely, you will have students whose

- Reading and writing abilities range from nonreaders to accomplished readers and writers
- English-speaking abilities and communication skills range from non-English speakers or hesitant English speakers to refined articulate English speakers
- Learning abilities range from learners with various learning disabilities to learners with few or no disabilities; to learners who are gifted and talented and combinations of abilities
- Attention span and emotions range from highly distracted to highly focused
- Knowledge and experiences in all areas of the curriculum range from no background to advanced experiences, multiple applications, and extended connections
- Cultural diversity and family configurations range in every way possible; family success and interest in school range from marginally absent and pained to highly rewarding and exciting

As soon as you can get to know your learners, you can begin tailoring your performance-based assessments to your learners, balancing motivation and engagement with the curriculum and instruction.

Know the Reasons for Selecting Your Assessments . . .

If there is one essential nugget of information to be mined from this chapter, it is the importance of knowing *why* you are doing what you are doing. First, you select assessments that supply the numbers and tell the stories that you are seeking for ongoing accountability. Second, you develop your year-long curriculum and instruction to show that you are planning the appropriate variety of evidence to substantiate your evaluations. Third, you select the kinds of assessments that invite, ignite, and excite the learning and learners, the teaching and teacher, and the curriculum and community for overall accountability. In these ways, you will be successful in measuring, deciding, and communicating learner achievement.

It may be helpful for you at this time to read the Standards for Teacher Competence in Educational Assessment of Students found in Appendix A.

Extend With Questions and Activities

Frequently Asked Questions

1. Assessment is extremely important. How can I assess my learners properly?

Each teacher develops a unique approach to assessment, evaluation, and accountability. You want to be you. After all, you teach who you are. This text will share many different ideas that you are encouraged to incorporate into your repertoire to enrich your classroom and career, expand your preparation and practices, and enhance your success and satisfaction.

2. Why do teachers use the terms *assessment, evaluation,* **and** *accountability* **interchangeably?**

Many teachers have not studied performance-based assessments closely, and they simply do not realize that the three terms differ in meaning and purpose. You will strengthen your teaching expertise, your learners will demonstrate greater achievement, and your communications with learners and family members will benefit when you clarify the terms and practices.

3. How can I be sure that I know the purposes for my assessment systems, evaluation practices, and accountability methods, and I am using the right one?

Try some "teacher self-talk." That means just like it sounds. Pretend you are teaching your learning experience to yourself. Can you clearly identify the assessment, evaluation, and accountability associated with your teaching, learning, and the learning experience? Does each area make sense to you? Here is a little secret: You want your assessment systems, evaluation practices, and accountability methods to be *visible, viable,* and *valuable.* That means, everyone should be able to see (visible) how you are going to monitor each learner's progress during and after the learning and check each learner's outcomes. The assessment systems should be appropriate and practical (viable). And, all assessment systems, evaluation practices, and accountability methods must be important (valuable).

Activities

1. Reflect on your own middle-level and/or secondary school learning experiences and the various practices of performance-based assessments that teachers asked you to do. Which ones did you think were appropriate and fair? Why did you feel this way? Then, which assessments did you think were inappropriate and perhaps unfair? Why did you feel this way? Write a few sentences in response to each question.

2. Show a colleague the practices of assessments that you liked and the practices of assessments that you disliked. Discuss the features of each kind.

3. Identify an objective for one learning experience you are planning to teach soon. Connect it to a practice of assessment, then to a system of evaluation, and, finally, to a method of accountability. Are your choices the most effective and efficient ones?

4. Select a unit of learning you are going to teach. Identify examples of feedback and data you would like to collect. Now relate your example with the basic concepts about performance-based assessments to understand the concepts and put them into practice.

2

Planning Assessments to Promote Understanding

Effective assessments involve an ongoing exchange of understanding between and among the teacher and the learners. You want to be sure that all of your learners "get it." In exchange, you want to be sure that you know *what* your learners get and *how* they get it. This exchange is called "reciprocity," in that the learners are led and inspired by the teacher while simultaneously the teacher is led and inspired by the learners. As the teacher, you must be ready to reteach or revise your teaching if and when your students do not "get it" or understand the knowledge, skills, and dispositions right away. And you must be ready to intervene, correct, and/or redirect their learning when they need assistance.

Not every teacher operates like this or welcomes reciprocal learning (Smyth, 2005). Many teachers consider an effective learning environment as one in which the teacher leads the class by delivering content, demanding participation, describing discoveries, and drawing conclusions for the students; learners are limited in their direct engagement or individual contributions in the classroom and in their connections to their personal lives and other learning. In these classrooms, the learning is more about the students following the teacher. However, through the practice of reciprocity, or the exchange of ideas and energies, the teacher remains open and receptive to understanding, innovation, and change that transform the learning, teaching, and schooling. True reciprocity benefits both learners and teachers, so let's explore these concepts and practices in greater detail.

Use Formal and Informal Assessments

You will collect data (before, during, and after the learning and teaching) by reading written assignments, giving quizzes and tests, observing, listening to responses, asking questions, giving tasks that learners perform in many different ways, and so forth. You will collect data in ways that are both formal and informal. *Formal assessments include assessments that learners generally are prepared to complete and are aware of the expectations associated with the assessments.* Expectations include, but are not limited to, the date of an assessment, the format or how an assessment will be conducted; how to prepare for the assessment; the technique or how the assessment will be scored, perhaps using a checklist or a rubric; and the communication or how the scores or feedback will be used.

Conversely, *informal assessments include observations, conversations, and interactions that contribute to your understanding of individual learners in various situations.* Generally, learners do not realize that they are being assessed. In some situations you may combine formal and informal assessments.

For example, at the start of the school year or during the introduction of a new unit of learning, you might administer a written assessment asking learners to select the best answer to a few questions about the digestive system. Additionally, you might show a model of the digestive system to three or four students sitting a side table and ask each of the students to identify a specific item in the model, one at a time. Each of these assessments constitutes the formal portion of the assessment.

Or you might show the model of the digestive system to the entire class and invite learners to volunteer in answering questions you pose about the model. You could encourage students to ask questions that would be posed back to the class or of you. These interactions are examples of informal assessments that permit you to gain an informal sense of knowledge and inspire students' interest in learning about the digestive system.

As you collect assessment data before, during, and after the learning and teaching, you will begin to rely more on formal assessments. Formal assessments address your goals and objectives using standardized checklists or rubrics so you can compare and contrast learners' outcomes with your expectations, learners' individual growth, and group progress. The most effective and efficient approaches for collecting assessment data combine formal and informal assessments.

For example, at the conclusion of the learning and teaching, teachers usually administer a formal assessment, such as a written vocabulary or math test. After scoring the assessment, you might sit with an individual student to ask him or her to explain the thinking behind incorrect or incomplete answers or why items were skipped. This sequence of events combines formal and informal assessments to document assessment data. With these insights, you can identify misconceptions or missed steps and plan a new learning experience on the given objectives.

Reflect on Understanding

Both formal and informal assessments entail the idea of understanding. When you facilitate a learning experience, you want every one of your students to "get it" or to understand

1. *What* is being taught to them, whether it is new or reviewed knowledge

2. *How* to use or interact with the knowledge as an important skill

3. *Why* knowledge is important or beneficial, and *Why* people think and express various viewpoints or perspectives associated with the knowledge and skills

To understand means to *acquire* a body of information, to *apply* the information to a variety of environments and practices, and to *appreciate* the information within a multitude of contexts. Too often, teachers focus on comprehension limited to isolated facts and figures without guiding their students in achieving complete understanding.

Understanding should be authentic, natural, and holistic, so students can construct their own meanings and connect the learning to their own lives in the classroom, throughout all of their classrooms, and out into the world (Brooks & Brooks, 1993). These three elements of acquisition, application, and appreciation related to knowledge, skills, and dispositions in multiple contexts must be present at all times if you want your learners to "get it."

It will be helpful if you consider each academic subject area that you teach. The knowledge associated with the particular subject area includes the conceptual understandings and content information communicated through the *cognitive domain* (Bloom, 1956; Bruner, 1966; Dewey, 1997; Piaget, 1990). The skills associated with the subject area include the applied processes and various practices demonstrated through the *psychomotor domain* (Simpson, 1972). The dispositions associated with the subject area also include the developed attitudes and array of outlooks demonstrated through the *affective domain* (Kohlberg, 1958; Krathwohl, Bloom, & Masia, 1964) and *psychosocial domains* (Bandura, 1989; Vygotsky, 1934/1980). Total understanding for particular subject area within a discipline or across the curriculum involves all four domains of learning occurring concomitantly. Not only will teach through all four domains, you will assess your learners using all four domains (see Appendix B).

When you are teaching new and possibly abstract concepts to your learners, remember that understanding does not occur in a vacuum. Find common references and concrete models, especially prior learning experiences, recent events, and physical artifacts to make the concept real. Give your learners tangible examples that they can touch and relate to their lives. Help your learners to sift through illustrations or patterns to differentiate between what something *is* as well as what it *isn't*. Encourage your learners to talk among themselves to share their inquiries, observations, experiences, and discoveries, with plenty of opportunities to explain new ideas to one another. Your learners are the best teachers, and they will benefit greatly when you let them teach one another. They can establish more clarity and understanding with one another than you can ever hope to accomplish.

Conduct Assessments at Multiple Times

For every lesson or learning experience that you create, you specify an objective. Most likely, your objective fulfills one or more learning expectations found in the state academic documents that match your school district's curriculum guide. The objectives may be drawn from your own academic subject area, or they may connect across several different subject areas as you integrate the curriculum and instruction.

The more familiar you are with your students' prior knowledge and personal experiences, the better prepared you will be able to create learning experiences that are developmentally appropriate for your students. You glean this information by assessing your learners before you teach your learning experience. Assessments conducted prior to introducing or teaching new information are called *preassess-ments*. The processes of collecting baseline data also are called conducting *entry-level assessments.*

Consider the term "baseline data" like the terms used with medical records. Adults are urged to gather and record personal health information before aging, getting sick, or beginning an intervention such as medicine or therapy. Information gathered prior to changes or intervention is called *baseline data.*

When you collect baseline data in your classroom, you may discover that your students are not ready for the learning experience you have designed, indicating that you must teach additional learning experiences to bridge from the unknown to the known, or you need to add additional background. As a result, you revise the learning experience you have written, or you construct a totally new learning experience. You gain these insights only when you collect appropriate baseline data.

Once you begin facilitating the new learning experience, you will monitor your learners' progress throughout the instruction. Assessments conducted before and during the teaching collect *formative data.* Formative data help you to organize your knowledge about the learners and the learning experience. The processes of collecting formative data also are called conducting *progress-monitoring assessments.*

Both entry-level preassessments and progress-monitoring assessments are known as *formative assessments.* They take place while learners are becoming proficient in new areas of the learning, as opposed to assessments that occur at the end of a unit, when learners demonstrate their levels of mastery of the identified objectives.

As you facilitate instruction, formative assessment data help you realize that you need to modify or revise the planned learning experience. Likewise, the data may help you discover some gaps that you need to fill or some overlaps that you can skip. You can change or add to the learning experience and continue to collect formative data as your learning experience unfolds.

After the learning experience is complete, you assess your learners again. Assessments conducted after the learning and teaching collect *summative data.* The assessments often include large amounts of content or sets of skills. These types of assessments frequently become formal processes and are considered "high stakes," as the outcomes indicate successful completion of a unit, course, or grade level. The processes of collecting summative data also are called conducting *concluding* or *final assessments.*

The purpose of assessment is to provide you and your learners with meaningful feedback. The preassessment or baseline data guide your planning before instruction; the formative assessment data frame your delivery and monitor your learners' progress during instruction; and the summative data conclude the learning after the teaching.

Figure 2.1 presents a graphic organizer to help you visualize the process.

Figure 2.1   Timing of Assessment Cycle

1. Preassessments	2. Formative Assessments	3. Summative Assessments
Collecting baseline or entry-level data prior to the learning and teaching; data should be kept to compare and contrast with formative assessment data and summative assessment data	Collecting progress-monitoring data conducted before or during the learning and teaching; data should be revisited frequently to adjust the teaching and learning	Collecting concluding or final data conducted at the end of the learning and teaching; data should be revisited occasionally throughout the course of study or school year

Consider All Kinds of Evidence

Whether you are organizing a single learning experience or an extended unit of learning, you should gather all kinds of evidence before, during, and after the learning. Think of this strategy in terms of preparing a trip. Before you travel, you decide where you are going, how you will get there, who will go with you, whom you will visit, what you will tour, and the kinds of activities that you'll pursue. You also determine how much money you can spend, the clothing that you'll need, and the equipment you want to take with you, along with the maps and information that you will need and the reservations and arrangements you will need to make. Some of your trip coordination will be imaginative and some of it will be practical. Overall, you want the trip to be organized, engaging, and rewarding. Preassessment works just the same way.

As the teacher, you need to determine where you going, how you will get there, and who will go with you so the classroom activities are organized, engaging, and rewarding. To accomplish these three objectives, you should preassess or take stock of the six components of assessment: learners and learning, teacher and teaching, the curricular content, and the classroom context; then you are ready to plan the learning and teaching with all kinds of evidence or data.

As you travel on your trip, you conduct all kinds of formative assessments. You notice if you are traveling on time, in comfort, going to the places and doing the things you expected. Frequently you have to check your plans or itinerary and you notice when new, pleasantly surprising events occur. Along the way, you modify your plans when desired or necessary.

When you return from the trip, you share your travels through photographs, artifacts, and tales with your family and friends. This is your summative assessment. You decide if you would travel to this same location again or if you would like to take a similar trip to another location. You build upon this knowledge and experience before you embark on your next adventure. Your preassessments, formative assessments, and summative assessments provide you with a wealth of feedback or data.

Become a Data-Driven Teacher

All of your assessments should be data driven. That means you can prove the outcomes by collecting a variety of information via a variety of forms. However, there are only three avenues through which you can collect your data: observing, listening, and reading. You will observe your learners and conduct conversations both in class and out of class formally and informally. You will read countless pieces of paper. All of these assessments are performance based and produce important evidence. To develop high-quality assessments, ask yourself the questions shown in Table 2.1.

Table 2.1   10 Questions to Guide Your Approaches to Assessments

How Well Does Your Assessment...
1. Fulfill the national, state, and school district standards and expectations?
2. Align with your curriculum and instruction?
3. Build on learners' prior learning and personal experiences?
4. Motivate learners to engage in the learning?
5. Encourage learners to construct new understandings?
6. Allow learners to learn together?
7. Connect across the curriculum and into the community?
8. Offer voice, choice, and agency?
9. Generate multiple forms of expression with authentic processes and products?
10. Showcase shared and exchanged outcomes?

You want to measure the evidence and competency (for assessment) to determine your decisions and directions (for evaluation) and report the outcomes and implications (for accountability). Teachers in data-driven classrooms maintain records for baseline data, formative data, and summative data that balance quantitative and qualitative measures analyzed for immediate feedback and for long-range planning. It is essential for classroom teachers to acquire a data-driven frame of mind and to let assessments be your friends.

Please notice that the word *data* is the plural form of the word *datum,* a word rarely used in classrooms or education. Too many educators use the word *data* incorrectly. You want to be competent and confident in your position as a professional educator, so you might want to practice saying, "The data are . . ."

Data include measurements and observations that may be numerical, descriptive, and/or representative. Data are facts, figures, information, statistics, records, images, and illustrations related to a person, place, thing, or event. For example, when you report how many students are in attendance, you are reporting data. You measure whether the student is in class or not in class. Throughout the school day, you notice which students are more and less actively engaged. You record some notes. Now you observe a pattern of behavior.

These patterns describe two different kinds of data related to attending: physically attending class and intellectually attending to task. Physically attending involves getting one's body to class, regularly, and on time. Intellectually attending involves engaging one's mental, emotional, and social connections. Both kinds of data are necessary as you preassess. In each situation, you note the progress, if and when you need to reteach all or part of the learning experience, and if and when the expectations have been achieved and need to be rewarded. You will also need to explore the reasons and patterns related to each category of not attending.

Balance Quantitative Data With Qualitative Data

These two kinds of assessments exemplify quantitative data and qualitative data. *Quantitative measurements produce data using numerical values.* Typically they are reported as numbers, percentages, time, tables, charts, and graphs. Many people in education prefer gathering evidence and reporting assessments as numbers. Quantitative data are frequently used when grading papers and scoring tests.

You need to be extremely careful as to what the measurements are measuring and what the numbers are reporting. The data may tell you the number of items that a learner got correct on an assignment or test, such as 7 out of 10, or 70 percent of the items. This information may be satisfactory for your purposes. However, the quantitative data do not tell you which items are correct and which ones are not correct. These data do not tell you if the score was an acceptable score or an unacceptable score for either this particular learner or in relationship to the class, other classes, prior classes, and so forth. These data also do not tell you how the learner got the correct items and if understanding has occurred. These data simply report that a learner got 7 out of 10 items correct.

Quantitative data often create more questions than answers. Once you start to discuss a student's learning patterns and outcomes with a professional colleague or family member, you will realize how much more you want to assess.

Qualitative measurements produce data using narrative descriptions, such as words or images. Typically, qualitative data are based on observations and conversations; they are reported as descriptive written passages, sounds, or pictures. Qualitative data help you understand the quantitative data telling you how and why an event occurred. Qualitative data assist you in noticing reoccurring commonalities and patterns for equipping you to make important judgments and predictions. Although all educators rely heavily upon qualitative data, they tend to be unsure of how to collect, report, and use qualitative data accurately in their classrooms.

Qualitative data allow you to organize assessments, especially preassessments and formative assessments like observations and informal conversations that are purposeful and meaningful yet not quantitative. Through interactions with your learners as individuals and groups, you organize the qualitative data. Your organization includes selecting, prioritizing, focusing, simplifying, and condensing qualitative data so they are manageable. For instance, returning to our previous example, let's say every learner in the class gets 7 out of 10 items correct. Some questions should jump at you. Did all the learners get the same 7 items correct?

And what does getting 7 out of 10 mean? Is that proficient? Were some items harder or easier than other items? Do you need to rewrite some items? Do you need to reteach some items?

All of these questions require you to gather qualitative data to analyze the situation. Numbers cannot and never tell the whole story. Yet, please keep in mind that you cannot spend all of your time and energy dissecting one assignment. Throughout all of your assessments, the secret is to seek a balance in your quantitative and qualitative data gathering.

Itemize Criterion-Referenced Assessments

Most of your assessments will be criterion referenced, whether they are administered before, during, or after the learning and teaching. *Criterion-referenced assessments compare and contrast outcomes with a list of expectations or criteria that, it is hoped, you communicate with your students during the learning and teaching.* As you assess, you are noting each student's level of achievement related to the criteria you have identified as important for the learning experience or unit.

When you preassess and gather baseline data, most likely you have not yet communicated the learning expectations for the learning experience, lesson, or unit to your students. You want to collect evidence to help you develop your curricular content, instructional practices, and assessment procedures. During preassessment, you also are getting a sense of the students' prior experiences and excitement about the upcoming learning experience or unit.

Here are some examples of criterion-referenced assessments. You plan to teach a social studies unit of learning to tenth graders on democracy. You identify a list of five learning expectations taken from the state academic standards and your school district's curricular scope and sequence guide. You decide what you are going to teach, what the students are going to do to be involved with the content, and the ways your students will communicate their learning both during the unit and at the end of the unit. These items become your criteria, so your assessments are criterion referenced. You will compare and contrast each learner's progress with the five expectations.

During the preassessment, you gather baseline data related to what your learners know, do, and believe related to democracy and the criteria that you have selected. You may discover that your students have already covered your five identified learning expectations. Or you may realize that this is a new topic for them to study. Generally, you will find that your learners share a wide range of knowledge, skills, and dispositions.

You need to collect the baseline data and start anecdotal records. Then you have notes to reference as you progress through the learning and teaching. Techniques for involving your learners in establishing the criteria, writing the rubrics, making choices, and exchanging their outcomes with one another are detailed in Chapter 3.

From a teacher:

When I plan a thematic unit, I think of the criteria in terms of the learners' knowledge, skills, and dispositions so they will become well-rounded individuals. I list all of the criteria and develop the unit highlighted with one or two major projects. Then I can assess the learners' outcomes before, during, and after the teaching and learning.

Describe Norm-Referenced Assessments

In middle-level and secondary school classrooms, occasionally you will use norm-referenced assessments, but you will use them far less often than criterion-referenced assessments. *Norm-referenced assessments involve a predetermined list of items and levels of outcomes comparing and contrasting learners' achievements with those of similar learners in other locations, that is, the state, nation, and world.* Standardized tests are the most common example of norm-referenced assessments in most schools today. Most middle-level and secondary school administrators guide their teachers through their own processes of communicating results related to standardized testing with learners and families.

However, many teachers use norm-referenced assessments every day without even realizing it. Without adequately planning the assessment to align with the curriculum and the instruction, teachers pose inquiries, organize activities, and make assignments, then leap into their assessments, score outcomes, and give feedback prior to establishing the anticipated levels of proficiency. These assessments become norm referenced, as teachers compare and contrast their learners' outcomes with one another rather than against a predetermined list of criteria. Students will be confused, parents will be disturbed, and you will be standing on thin ice. You want to avoid administering formative or summative assessments that become norm referenced only because of your lack of preparation.

You can use norm-referenced assessments as a pretest to collect the baseline data; and at times, norm-referenced assessments can be fascinating in that you can see how your learners relate to other learners. However, too often, teachers want to use norm-referenced assessments as a definitive reflection of the teaching, learning, and schooling. Try to keep norm-referenced assessments to a minimum, yet value them for their benefits.

Understand Assessment Principles and Practices

Assessment is an academic field accompanied by its own researched principles and practices. Most likely, you have heard many of these assessment terms. It is important for you to examine the terminology closely so you can place them into your own teaching context and use them appropriately with your students, their families, and your colleagues. It is helpful to connect the terminology to one of your own assessments as you proceed.

Rationalize Validity and Reliability

Validity in assessment means you are asking learners to demonstrate outcomes that correspond directly to the objectives. For an assessment to be valid, it must fit your intention and apply to the learning. You have to be able to rationalize

1. The expectations and outcomes you are assessing. This is called *content validity:* your assessments match the curriculum and instruction.

2. The ways you are assessing the outcomes. This is called *criterion validity:* your assessments anticipate the learner's degree of success.

3. The reasons you are assessing outcomes in the ways you have selected. This is called *construct validity:* your assessments showcase the purposes for learning.

First, look at your assessments to see if they have *face validity,* that is, the assessments appear to satisfy the requirements associated with construct, criterion, and construct validity. Second, examine your assessments closely to see if your assessments have *consequential validity,* that is, the learners' responses are useful. Then, once you have established validity, you can communicate much more clearly with your learners, their families, your colleagues, and your administrators.

Here is an example. When you are preassessing your learners' math computation skills in algebra, most likely you administer a written assessment with a series of approximately 10 problems ranging in difficulty. Your preassessment might also include one or two written problems for you and your students, to gather baseline data related to this particular skill.

In order for you to establish validity in this assessment, you need to be sure that the assessment is assessing the knowledge (what students need to know), the skills (how students demonstrate or show knowledge), and the dispositions (why learners are learning the identified outcomes connected to the world around them). The results from a valid assessment should provide you with valuable information that guides your planning and teaching.

Your assessments will be valid only if they are reliable. *Reliability in assessment means you can depend on the assessment you have selected to give you a consistent range of results every time.* You want to know that

1. The kind of assessments you are using will give you the information you need to make wise decisions regarding the teaching, learning, and schooling. This is called *stability reliability:* your assessments generate consistent outcomes with repeated uses over time.

2. Multiple versions of the same assessment will produce the same results. This is called *alternate form stability:* any of your assessments for a particular learning experience or unit of learning will show the same distribution of outcomes.

3. You are using the most reliable kinds of assessment so the learning and teaching are both effective and efficient. This is called *internal consistency:* your assessments actually work.

These measurements are especially vital during preassessment, as you want to gather evidence and data that you can use to compare and contrast data related to current knowledge, skills, and dispositions with formative and summative assessment data.

Here is an example. When you are preassessing knowledge, skills, and dispositions for a unit in science about the geologic formations, you want to organize your assessment tool so you gather data that pertains specifically to the topic and your expectations. Your assessment tool will be reliable if you gather the same array of results every time you administer this particular assessment tool. You can compare and contrast preassessment data with formative data with summative data. The same assessment tool can be used each time.

You also want to be able to use the same assessment tool every time you get ready to teach this particular unit of learning. So, year after year, you administer this same assessment focused on the geologic formations. If it is reliable, it should work every time. The assessment will be dependable and trusted; your time and efforts will be effective and efficient.

Both validity and reliability are measured in degrees of achievement; they are not all-or-nothing measurements. *And validity is more important than reliability.* If your assessments are valid, they will be reliable. However, if your assessments are reliable, they may not be valid. It is easy to infer validity. Let's examine these statements closely. To be *valid* is to produce results that fit the objectives. However, to be *reliable* means the assessment will consistently produce the same range of results every time. Your assessment may be reliable yet produce a range of results that do not fit with your objectives. Your results are consistent, but consistently unusable.

Ensure Salience, Fidelity, and Robustness

It is essential to place validity and reliability in the context of your own teaching principles and practices as established among the basic concepts of performance-based assessments introduced in Chapter 1.

Therefore, you want your assessments to ensure salience. *Salience means you are assessing that which is important and relevant.* Your learning experiences and units will cover a great amount of information. You have to decide the knowledge, skills, and dispositions that you want to emphasize the most and that, one hopes, your learners will retain. You will identify the items that are salient and select strategies that will help your students to understand the salient portions of your learning experiences and units. Ultimately, you want to be able to describe the assessment, that is, tell what it is; justify its purpose, that is, tell how you are using it; and explain its significance, that is, tell why you chose it.

Simultaneously, you want your assessments to have fidelity and robustness. *Fidelity means you are using assessments that learners can understand and consider* fair related to the assessment, expectations, scoring, and feedback. *Robustness means you are using assessments that incorporate adequate depth, breadth, and opportunity for learners to express themselves* and provide enough evidence for you to be sure they "get it."

Separate Objectivity From Subjectivity

One of your greatest challenges is being objective or fair to the best of your ability. *Fairness means your assessments are bias free.* Your assessments must be developed so that all learners can comprehend the context and expectations so they can do well academically and socially. You want to ask questions and assign activities with all the necessary information and instructions communicated clearly and completely. All of your students need to be prepared and equipped to understand the content, the assigned expectations, and the forms of assessment. Most of the time, you can remain objective when you are analyzing the results of formal assessments.

There should be no surprises for anyone. You want to develop assessments that give all learners a chance to succeed, with no discrimination based on race/ethnicity, gender, social class, abilities/ disabilities, language, religion, cleanliness, and so forth. As middle-level and secondary school students age, some of them become more anxious, frightened, even angry about completing assessments. Some parents have created additional stress for their children by setting high, if not unreasonable, standards for them. And some students may have lost hope that their teachers will like and help them.

For example, when you administer a written assignment or test, you score the responses, and you give the assignment a score. Using multiple choice, matching, or true/false questions helps you to maintain objectivity, as does selecting answers on a prepared document or typing answers on the computer. You can even tell your students to write their names on the backs of their papers so you can't see their names when you're reading their papers. Or you can ask your learners to select fictitious names or a secret codes to write on their papers and to keep the fictitious name or secret code in a special place so you do not know the author of each paper.

However, there are three essential caveats for you to note related to objectivity:

1. Shortly after the school year begins, you will know your learners' individual forms of expression and avenues of thinking, especially when learners prepare their papers using their own handwriting.

2. All people do not learn the same way, express themselves the same ways, value the same content equally, and/or process material the same ways. Although all of the students in your classroom may be within a year or two of the same age and live in the surrounding neighborhoods, they will differ from one another in many ways. You must collect baseline data from each learner in order to teach each one effectively as individuals while also members of a group. You want to discover your students' needs and interests, to empower them with every tool you can share specific to their needs and interests, and to give them as much academic freedom as each student can handle. Ultimately, you must try to individualize the learning, teaching, and assessments as much as possible.

3. You can't always be fair. Some of your learners will understand the content and demonstrate the skills exhibiting basic levels of proficiency, and some learners will exhibit advanced levels of proficiency. Some of your learners will be more challenged with parts of the curriculum, the learning process, or maybe with just about everything related to school. Some students receive much more help and support at home. You cannot weigh the processes and products reflecting each of your students using the same assessment. Your students are not the same. No matter how hard you, they, and their families try to help some learners, not all learners are going to perform as well as other learners.

Subjectivity is a sensitive subject, yet every teacher, parent, and supervisor incorporates it into their feedback and assessments. *Subjectivity in classrooms generally means the willingness to look at partial work or how the task was completed or the problem was solved, considering the amount of effort that was dedicated to the outcome with resulting achievement, allowing for some "wiggle room," and giving the benefit of the doubt.*

For example, when you are grading math problems, you might ask your learners to show their work so you can follow their thinking and reward correct attempts. When you give feedback on short stories, each student is considered in the context of his or her individual past abilities and current potential. If the learners show progress or improvement, you might interpret or acknowledge the effort even when the product is incomplete. You modify your expectations based on individual capabilities in terms of language development, special education needs, and so forth. Modifications may be objective and/or subjective. Most teachers try to minimize the subjectivity and concentrate on the objectivity associated with their performance-based assessments.

Watch for Common Errors in Assessing

As you embark into this adventure in learning about performance-based assessments, let's consider errors frequently made by classroom teachers.

1. Teachers tend to assess the knowledge, skills, and dispositions that they understand and value. This error matches the trend

that teachers tend to teach what they understand and value, substantiating the condition known as the "generational perpetuation of practice" (Gallavan, 2007).

2. Teachers do not use the most appropriate assessment. This tendency occurs because teachers may not be aware of the wealth of choices available to them. Known as the "poverty of practice" (Black & Wiliam, 1998), teachers tend to continue using what they have seen and always used gleaned through their "observation of apprenticeship" (Lortie, 1975).

3. Teachers tend to assess too many items at one time. Outcomes are grouped together as papers, presentations, projects, and portfolios receiving one overall score or grade; the feedback lacks specificity and direction for the student, parents, teacher, and school.

4. Teachers tend to assess unfairly. Teachers may or may not recognize this significant error. Teachers' errors occur as a result of

   a. *Generosity:* Giving selected learners higher scores than actually earned

   b. *Punishment:* Giving selected learners lower scores than actually earned

   c. *Prejudice:* Giving selected learners inadequate or incorrect information and preparation for an assessment

   d. *Central tendencies:* Giving midpoint scores too often (frequently occurs at the start of the school year or semester until teachers become better acquainted with their students)

   e. *Halo effect:* Giving scores based on the learner's overall record of achievement and/or the teacher's attitude toward the student

   f. *Pygmalion theory,* also called the "self-fulfilling prophecy": Giving scores indicating how well learners do when you are present after you have shared with them how well you think and believe they will do

   g. *Misinterpretation of scores:* Not understanding how to disaggregate the data and conduct an item analysis to construct a complete and accurate analysis of each individual learner as well of the whole group

   h. *Misuse of scores or manipulating scores intentionally:* Placing students in groups, referring to special services, and communicating outcomes incorrectly to learners, parents, and colleagues

Realize that unlimited variables impact the learning, teaching, and schooling; you want to understand and control all of the variables the best you can.

Visualize the Overall Process . . .

Remember the overall assessment, evaluation, and accountability processes that were shown in Figure 1.3 in Chapter 1. As you develop a single learning experience or an expanded unit of learning with several objectives, you want each objective to match a particular assessment. As your unit progresses, you record the assessments until it is time to evaluate the overall outcomes. Then you report the progress in some method for accountability. The information in the next chapters will guide you through these processes and provide you with authentic classroom examples.

Extend With Questions and Activities

Frequently Asked Questions

1. Which assessments should I plan in advance of teaching a unit or learning experience?

You want to plan aspects of all three assessments (the preassessments, formative assessments, and summative assessments) in advance and to make sure that the aspects are aligned with one another to monitor progress and outcomes. The more detailed your data are, the more efficient your teaching and the more effective your learners' understanding of the concepts, processes, and outlooks in multiple contexts will become.

2. What is one way to align all of my assessments?

Select your goals and objectives from your state curricular standards and student learning expectations. Your school district might publish a curriculum scope and sequence chart, too, that you should consult. Ask your students to demonstrate their understanding of a particular concept, process, or outlook at the beginning of the unit or learning experience to collect baseline data, during the unit to collect formative data, and then at the conclusion of the unit to collect summative data. If you are consistent, then the data should reveal growth trends during the unit.

3. How can I be as fair as possible?

There are three words that will help you here: *authentic, natural,* and *holistic.* You want to use assessments that match the learning as closely as possible. Give your learners opportunities to answer these questions, solve these problems, or conduct these tasks or similar ones to prepare for the assessments. Your aim is not to teach to the assessment; your aim is to equip your students with the understanding necessary to document anticipated achievement.

Activities

1. Identify an area of subject matter that you understand. Select some of the key knowledge, skills, and dispositions that you consider critical to understanding the area of subject matter. It is important that you identify the information, application, and appreciation. Give reasons why your selections of information, applications, and appreciation unify and strengthen the understanding of the subject matter.

2. Consider the four domains: cognitive, psychomotor, social, and affective. Specify a different body of subject matter and give examples of each of the four domains.

3. Provide one example of quantitative data and one example of qualitative data that are essential for you to document and communicate with parents for one subject area that you teach.

4. Develop an example of validity and an example of reliability relevant to subject matter that you teach to help you distinguish the differences and to incorporate them into your assessments.

5. Consider your teaching style and classroom management systems. Set three goals to help you to be and stay fair in the ways you assess your learners.

3

Collecting Baseline
Data for Preassessments

Perhaps you consider assessment to be the end point to your teaching. Many teachers approach assessment as the finale, when they see whether their learners "got it" by giving written tests, recording the grades, and moving on to the next learning experience (lesson plan) or unit. Too often, tests are administered with few or no opportunities for the teacher or students to connect outcomes with the content and the real world. These teachers rarely revisit or reteach the expectations. Their assessments seem to be given in isolation from the learning, the teaching, or the schooling.

Assessments are highly informative and continuous processes that occur before, during, and after the learning and teaching. When you assess before the learning, you preassess the learners' entry levels. Preassessment baseline processes and data are integral to effective learning and teaching; this chapter is dedicated entirely to helping you and your learners start on a solid foundation.

Set Three Goals to
Guide Your Preassessments

During preassessment, you gather baseline or entry-level data to accomplish three goals:

1. To acknowledge where to begin the learning for the whole class as well as for individual learners; this is assessment *as* learning

2. To plan where to begin the teaching; this is assessment *for* learning

3. To establish a foundation or basis of current knowledge, skills, and dispositions so you can note the progress you and your students achieve both during and after the learning and teaching; this is assessment *of* learning

Figure 3.1 can help you picture your preassessment goals.

Figure 3.1   Preassessment Goals

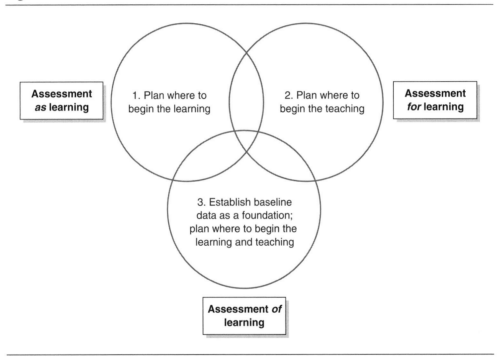

Before you begin planning or teaching, you want to allocate time and energy to preassessing your learners and the situation. It is essential that you take stock of the six components of assessment (refer to Figure 1.1 in Chapter 1) that contribute to the preparation, implementation, and closure of each learning experience.

Know Where to Begin the Learning

The first goal is to know where to begin the learning. You must consider each learner in relationship to each subject area that you teach. Some of your learners will demonstrate proficiencies that are rated as being on grade level, some learners are rated below the grade level, and some learners are rated above the grade. Your task is to preassess each student in each subject area so you know where to start your teaching to enhance their learning. For example, you may have planned to teach hyperboles when you discover that you need to start by reviewing or reteaching facts, opinions, literal descriptions, and figurative speech before you can begin delving into hyperboles. For teaching to be effective, you must assess the learners first.

Some learners remain in the same middle-level and secondary schools as they move through the grade levels. As the teacher, you have easy access to the students' permanent records, their previous teachers, and the students' families. These are three key resources for getting to know your learners. However, some students are new to your school and perhaps the school district. You may not have any access to the learners' permanent records or to their previous teachers. If this is your situation, you will want to visit with the student's parents as soon as you can to become better acquainted with the student and his or her past strengths and weaknesses.

From an experienced teacher:

I have a general blueprint that I have designed for the entire school year. My blueprint is based on the state standards and fits between what happens in algebra I and what happens in pre-calculus at our school. I preassess the learners in every subject as soon as they arrive so I can determine where they can start their learning and I can start my teaching. There is much to cover in Algebra II, and I don't have time to spend reteaching what they already know and can do. Reteaching can bore the learners, especially in high school.

Plan Where to Start Your Teaching

This second goal may seem obvious; however, it is more challenging than you may initially realize. As a middle-level and/or secondary school teacher, most likely you are responsible for teaching all of the subjects in one or two academic areas. The state curricular standards will stipulate specific student learning expectations for a particular grade level, so you can preview the range of knowledge, skills, and dispositions that encompass the grade level that you teach.

Now you can begin designing your instruction with a variety of learner-centered strategies to engage your students in mastering the curriculum. You can start gathering resources and activities to make the learning come alive. And you can begin aligning your assessments with the curriculum and instruction. However, you must consider the fit with the other two goals of preassessment before you can continue.

Establish a Foundation to Note Progress

Once that you have matched the learning with your teaching, you need to establish a foundation to note progress for each learner in each subject area. The only way you will know if you are making steady progress is to know where you began. This third goal is the most important goal in preassessment. You must conduct entry-level data gathering early in the school year or the unit of learning to accomplish three outcomes:

1. To compare and contrast the starting point with the ending point

2. To introduce and integrate new knowledge, skills, and dispositions to the learners that build upon prior knowledge, skills, and dispositions and connect with real-world experiences and other subject areas' curriculum and instruction

3. To cover and master all of the curricular standards and student learning expectations at your grade level in each subject area

Keeping these three outcomes in mind as you develop your preassessments will motivate you to develop the assessments that provide you with the clearest information.

Question Each of the Six Components of Assessment

From a teacher:

> *Preassessment is the key. Never assume that your learners do not know the information that you are planning to teach. Teachers are wasting way too much time maintaining this attitude. We should know what we are doing and as quickly as possible. That way we can cover much more and rapidly. Get organized and get going!*

It will be helpful for you to view the six components of assessment through the essential questions presented in Table 3.1. Ask yourself these questions as you consider your preassessments and gather your baseline data.

Table 3.1 Preassessment Questions for the Six Components of Assessment

Component of Assessment	Preassessment Questions
1. Each learner's individuality and background	a. What are the cultural characteristics of each learner? What are the cultural characteristics of the class as a whole? b. What are the learning styles of each learner? What are the learning styles of the class as a whole? c. What are the personal interests of each learner? What are the personal interests of the class as a whole?
2. Learner's prior knowledge and experiences	a. What does each student know, do, and believe related to the objective? What does the class know, do, and believe? b. What does each student want to learn related to the objective? What does the class want to learn? c. How does each student want to engage with the learning and with other learners to explore and express new learning?
3. Teacher's expertise and expectations	a. What is your expertise related to the content and processes? Do you have a favorite area or a special interest or skill? Do you have unique experiences to enhance and enrich the learning? b. What knowledge, skills, and dispositions do you want to be sure to teach during the learning experience or unit? c. What knowledge, skills, and dispositions do you want to be sure to integrate across the curriculum and to connect outside of the classroom?
4. Teacher's organization and readiness	a. What do you know about the objective? b. How do you want to facilitate the learning? What method do you prefer? c. What resources can you access to expand your expertise and readiness?
5. Curricular content and academic standards	a. How might you connect the learning expectations with the individual student's prior learning? b. How can you ensure that the learning is student centered, student directed, engaging and providing them with multiple ways to express their learning and exchange ideas? c. How might you make the learning meaningful and relevant?
6. Learning community context	a. How will you establish a community of learners in your classroom to connect with the objective? b. How might you connect learning expectations with the class? c. How might you connect student learning with the world around them?

Each of these questions will generate more questions that you will ask yourself as you make important decisions to inform and support effective learning and teaching. Try writing a few of your own questions, related to your favorite units and learning experiences, for each of the six components of assessment.

Gather Baseline Data

The information that you gather during the preassessment provides you with baseline data. *Baseline data describes the situation prior to the learning and teaching.* You cannot determine exactly where to begin the teaching and learning processes unless you have collected baseline data. For example, you might presume that since your learners are ninth graders you can begin the learning and teaching at the ninth grade level. This would be a huge error. Your ninth graders' achievement levels will range from learners who know nothing about your topic to learners who know a great amount and can readily apply the anticipated outcomes in many different situations.

Plus—and this is vital for your success—you cannot document, much less communicate, either your students' levels of individual progress and achievement or your own teaching levels of progress and achievement unless you know where the students start. In order to compare and contrast, it is strongly recommended that you preassess the final expectations before you begin.

You can collect preassessment or baseline data using every form of assessment that you will use during as well as after the learning and teaching. Your students' preassessment results will be written, spoken, and/or demonstrated to you in a variety of ways; you will want to select the most appropriate preassessments in light of the six components of assessment.

Table 3.2 provides some examples of effective preassessments for each of the six components of assessment.

Be Aware of Your Rating Reliability

Rating your assessment data requires you to realize your own rating reliability. During preassessments are the times to enhance your awareness of how you rate your learners' progress, before you begin collecting formative and summative feedback and data. Ask yourself these critical questions. Do you do your best to assess:

1. Using predetermined and public criteria?

2. Every learner using the same criteria and mindset?

Table 3.2   Examples of Preassessment for the Six Components of Assessments

Component of Assessment	Preassessment or Baseline Data
1. Each learner's individuality and background	• Pretest that matches the posttest • Individual conference • Writing sample
2. Learners' prior knowledge and experiences	• Cooperative learning group activity • Conversation in class • KWHL chart (what do you *know*, what do you *wonder*, and what are ways to find out *how* to learn followed later with what did you *learn*)
3. Teacher's expertise and expectations	• Prioritization of content • Prioritization of methods • Prioritization of resources
4. Teacher's organization and readiness	• Pretest that matches the posttest • Conversation in class • KWHL chart
5. Curricular content and academic standards	• Curricular mapping for one learning experience • Curricular mapping for a unit of learning • Curricular mapping that scaffold, spiral, and compact learning
6. Learning community context	• Technique for building community • Technique for connecting learning to prior learning • Technique for connecting learning to real world

3. Every process and product for one expectation using the same criteria and mindset?

4. All processes and products using similar criteria and mindset?

5. Similarly to other teachers on your team and in your school?

You want to refer to these questions frequently to check yourself. The goal is to remain as objective, fair, and transparent as possible. At some point, a student, parent, or administrator will challenge your ratings, and you want to be competent, confident, and ready in all you do.

Generate Preassessment Ideas

Many teachers like to preassess their learners (Inman & Tollefson, 2006), and it is imperative that you establish positive and productive habits for conducting preassessments early in your career. Preassessments can be conducted in any way that you teach or you check the learning. Table 3.3 presents a list to help you generate more ideas.

Investigate the Three Spheres Of Learning

When you preassess your learners, you want to preview the learning within three spheres of learning: cognitive, procedural, and situational (see Figure 3.2 and Table 3.4). Each sphere is unique and fulfills a different purpose in learning.

Table 3.3   Preassessment Ideas and Applications

Idea	*Sample Applications*
Analogies and metaphors	Announce to the class that the next unit of learning in social studies is about communities. Then take out a drawing of a saltwater fish tank. Point out the many different colorful fish, plants, and items found in the fish tank. Ask learners how a community is like a fish tank. (Everyone shares the same space, food, water, and air, but everyone is unique.) Explain the use of analogy and metaphor. You also can include allegory and similes.
Book and story discussions	After showing the cover of a book or reading the first few pages of the book aloud, ask learners if they have heard or read the book and to predict or forecast how the story will unfold.
Checklists	To introduce a learning experience with written math problems, post a checklist on the board or overhead projector. Ask students to insert the items on the checklist that one should follow in solving a written math problem.
Circle talks	In a circle with no more than five learners, ask each student to supply the next step in a sequence of events that occurred in the story they recently read as a group.
Conversations	Using appropriate questioning strategies (see Chapter 5), lead a conversation about the most recent science unit of learning.
Cooperative learning group activities	Place all learners in cooperative learning groups of no more than five students per group. After assigning jobs within the groups, ask groups to list examples of the next unit (transportation, weather, communication, geometry, nutrition, state history, and so forth).

Idea	Sample Applications
Demonstrations	Ask learners to solve a math problem on paper, individually with the teacher, or on the board for the whole class, identifying and explaining each step along the way.
Games	In cooperative learning groups, ask students to create a game to learn the weekly vocabulary words.
Graphic organizers	Ask each student to work with a partner to construct a graphic organizer that shows the steps in conducting a science experiment.
Independent reading records	Ask learners to record themselves individually reading orally into a tape recorder. Then ask each student to listen to his or her own reading and note errors on an independent prescribed reading record.
Independent reading responses	In a foreign language or literature class, after a set of partners has read the same passage silently, ask one partner to read the passage aloud, and ask the other partner to note reading errors on a prescribed record.
Individual or small group conferences	Meet with a group of no more than three students to ask the members of the group to tell what they know or to show what they can do related to a specific task (solve a math problem, write a paragraph, and so forth).
Interviews	Meet with one student at a time and ask her or him specific questions that will be asked individually of each student (definitions and uses of new vocabulary, math computations, pictures of science applications, map locations, and so forth).
Interest inventories	Give a list of items (for example, all the grade-level subject areas or ways to spend free time) to the entire class. Ask students to rate each item as high, medium, or low related to their individual interest in each item.
Journals	Ask learners to write a short passage about an event or a video. Review the passage for specific purposes.
Learner-led instructions	Ask learners to write the instructions for checking out a book from the library, playing a common game, making a peanut butter and jelly sandwich, and so forth.
Learner self-assessments	Ask students to correct a writing passage. Give each student a checklist of items to conduct a self-assessment that includes each expectation.

(Continued)

Table 3.3 (Continued)

Idea	Sample Applications
Math samples	Ask learners to complete a series of math samples that range in difficulty.
Mock problem solving	In cooperative learning groups, ask learners to solve a social interaction problem (getting along with other learners in the cafeteria, completing homework every day, communicating with parents, and so forth).
Nonlinguistic representations	Give each learner a list of symbols to identify either orally or in writing (street signs, math symbols, punctuation marks, and so forth).
Observations	Show the class a short video (for example, a popular cartoon) and ask them to share observations in small group discussions or in writing.
Parent consultations	Ask parents what they think their children will know or can do in a particular subject area (for example, reading, writing, or math).
Performances	Ask the learners to act out how they would respond in a particular situation (introducing family members at back-to-school night, seeking help in the library, asking another learner to be quiet, and so forth).
Pictures	Ask learners to draw a picture to illustrate a poem.
Portfolios	After completing a unit of learning in science or social studies, ask students to select three or four items to include in a portfolio to use for parent conferences and goal setting.
Quick checks	While introducing a new unit of learning, ask students intermittent questions as a quick check. (See questioning skills in Chapter 5.)
Reading samples	Give students a copy of a written passage and ask them to read the sample aloud individually so you can record reading levels.
Running records	From several oral reading samples, record the learners' strengths and weaknesses on running reading records.
Simulations	Create a set of situations related to crossing the United States in a covered wagon and record them on note cards. Ask groups of learners to act out or simulate their situations.

Idea	Sample Application
Skits	Ask groups of learners to demonstrate science concepts (how plants grow, how the Earth rotates and revolves, and so forth).
Surveys with rate and rank	Distribute a written survey on which learners rate items (high, medium, and low) and rank items (1 through 10, with 1 as the highest rank, related to personal preference or importance according to a known source).
Tasks	Ask learners to demonstrate a particular task with various levels of challenges attached to the task to assess levels of proficiencies (an athletic endeavor, a math skill, a writing skill, and so forth).
Teaching one another	In small groups of three to five students, provide each student with a note card with a word or a piece of information recorded on it. Each student teaches the other members of the small group the meaning or uses of the information written on the note card.
Testing	Distribute a written test with similar or the same information that you will be assessing in written form at the end of the upcoming learning experience and/or unit of learning.
Writing samples	After introducing a topic or issue, ask students to write a few words, sentences, or paragraphs related to the topic or issue from their own experiences or about imaginary experiences.

Figure 3.2   Three Spheres of Learning

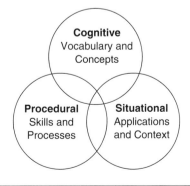

Table 3.4   Three Spheres of Learning

Sphere	Definition	Samples
Cognitive	Describing or showing one's thinking related to abstract concepts or big ideas as well as specific items or illustrative examples	Beliefs, impressions, information, interpretations, judgments, philosophies, samples, theories; for example: • Telling what a community is • Exhibiting good citizenship • Explaining why we need science
Procedural	Describing or showing one's understanding of a method, process, or skill	Demonstrations, illustrations, instructions, models, procedures, selections, steps; for example: • Completing the steps of math problems • Giving directions to a place on a map • Reading a passage aloud to the class
Situational	Describing or showing one's application of content and practices associated with a particular condition, context, or circumstance	Combinations of cognitive and procedural; for example: • Demonstrating the best moves while planning a sports events • Writing an appropriately succinct, cohesive, and correct paragraph or paper • Solving a written math problem utilizing the most efficient math equations

Keep Anecdotal Records

Intricate to your preassessment gathering of data is keeping anecdotal records. *Anecdotal records are your own observations and analyses of all six components of assessment.* Most likely, your records will be maintained in both formal and informal modes of organizations. Your anecdotal records will become your most insightful guidelines as you make decisions related to your curriculum, instruction, and classroom management.

Establish Formal Anecdotal Records

Formal anecdotal records include checklists, charts, and class rosters that you have organized and detailed for specific purposes. You might use a checklist to track who is responsible for various classroom tasks, with spaces to note how well each learner accomplished the task. You might use a seating chart to record who has responded to a question and how well she or he responded. And you might use a class roster to document who is late or absent, with spaces for explanation.

Here is a clever idea. Write each learner's name with a bold, colored marker along the bottom edge of a 4 × 6-inch note card. The writing should be about one-half inch high. Using tape that runs across the entire length of the upper edge of the card, layer the note cards and tape the them onto a clipboard so that you can see each learner's name below the previous card. Each card will flip up so you can write a note on the card. This is another kind of formal anecdotal record on which you can document progress, such as during oral reading. You can record the errors that each reader makes so you can be ready to teach, improve learner outcomes, and notice achievement.

Think about the kinds of accounting you need to maintain on your students so you can create a variety of checklists, charts, and class rosters to fulfill each purpose. Duplicate them on different colors of papers, and keep them in a three-ring binder so you can access the records quickly. Your formal anecdotal records will be necessary for you to be able to report data to school administrators, students, parents, and colleagues. You will want to be able to review and analyze the data in a scientific method as you prepare report forms at the end of the quarter.

Maintain Informal Anecdotal Records

Informal anecdotal records include assorted notes you make and collect throughout your school day. Your students, their parents, and your colleagues will share information with you all the time. Keep a notebook and a pen or pencil with you at all times. You might want to attach the pen or pencil to the notebook with a string so you can grab the set at once.

For example, when you are standing in the hallway monitoring learners or greeting your learners before the school day begins, frequently you will be told essential information, such as a learner is going to be absent due to a sporting event that day or there are papers in the office that you need to pick up so you can distribute them to your learners. A student may hand you an important note, perhaps from a parent, that requires your attention and possibly a response after the school day begins.

Interactions like these occur nonstop in schools, and you simply can't remember them all. Plus you need to keep every piece of correspondence note that you receive; file them in your records, and make note of how and when you responded. Organize a filing system with an individual file for each of your students. When you receive a written note from a learner or parent, place it in the student's file. If you respond to the note, photocopy your response and place the copy in the student's file. Be sure you write the date on the note and your response. You might want to create a chart to tape or staple on the left side of each learner's file where you can maintain a correspondence log. A correspondence log will help you if a parent claims you have not responded to a note or attended to a request. You can file all kinds of documents in the student's individual file, and if possible, you should keep the files in a locked file drawer. Many people will come and go in your classroom, and these files are confidential.

Follow These Guidelines as You Preassess

Here is a list of guidelines for you to keep in mind as you preassess:

1. *You need to preassess everything you teach.* This is the only way you will know where to start the learning and teaching; this is the only way you can note progress over time.

2. *There are many different ways to preassess.* Select the technique that will provide you with the information you need and want to start the learning and teaching.

3. *Select a preassessment that is developmentally appropriate, seeking a variety of related information* (see Chapter 7) *using a variety of assessment forms* (see Chapter 8). For example, if you want to know if your learners can use apostrophes, then select a preassessment that examines using and not using apostrophes in a variety of contexts and a variety of written passages.

4. *If your learners score well, most likely the preassessment is too easy or too limited in variety.* You want to be sure that you preassess seeking a variety of information and using a variety of assessment forms. Here is a suggestion: You can ask the five most difficult questions. If a learner answers 4 out of the 5 questions correctly, you do not need to reteach this information.

5. *If your learners score poorly, most likely the preassessment is too hard or too broad in variety.* You want to be sure that the learners

are comfortable and understand the form of assessment. However, most likely, you have not asked the right questions to help you.

6. *Select a preassessment that generates data can be compared and contrasted with data collected at the end of the learning and teaching* as part of the summative assessments.

7. *Not all preassessments are written.* A written preassessment can provide you with objective documentation that you can access throughout the learning and teaching to inform your formative assessments and to use at the conclusion as part of the summative assessments.

8. *If you administer preassessments that are not written, design a rubric or response sheet* (see Chapter 9) on which you can record answers to access both during and at the conclusion of the learning and teaching.

9. *Preassessments can be open ended* (see questioning strategies in Chapter 5) to provide you with a range of responses and insights about your students' needs and interests. From open-ended preassessments, you can amass many ideas that you can use to expand and enhance the learning and teaching.

10. *Keep copies of your preassessments,* not only to document the progress your learners and you have made during the school year, but to reference when you review your collections of assessments to help you improve your effectiveness through the years. Very quickly, you will detect trends that will help you become a better teacher that you can share with your department chair or school administrator. Professional reflections also can help you decide what areas of professional development you want to pursue.

Realize That Assessment Is a Continuous Process . . .

You may not have been aware of the power of preassessing to gather baseline data. This is the first and most important step in a continuous process. Once you have acquired the habit of preasssessing your learners, you will wonder how you ever managed without conducting this step. Your effectiveness will improve greatly and immediately. And you will enjoy your teaching much more.

Extend With Questions and Activities

Frequently Asked Questions

1. What can I use right away to start preassessing my learners?

Look at your goals and objectives (stemming from the state standards and student learning expectations). Collectively the goals and objectives fit within a body of content that includes knowledge, skills, and dispositions that your learners should know, do, and believe at the end of the learning. Think about your instructional strategies for delivering the content. When the instruction is concluded, you will check the learning in a way that matches the instruction. You can plan your aligned curriculum, instruction, and assessments prior to meeting your learners. Now select five of the questions on your assessment. These five questions serve as the preassessment.

2. What if the preassessment data show that my learners need to start in various places?

This result of preassessment is to be expected. You will make two important decisions. The first decision addresses the range of responses collected in the preassessment data. Group the responses to see if there are some emerging groups. You will have to decide if you can teach the anticipated content in groups so that all of your learners show adequate progress that is developmentally appropriate. If you have a few learners who demonstrate extreme strengths or weaknesses, you should consult with your grade-level colleagues and the special education team. Most likely, you will teach the content to groups or to the whole class with some slight modifications.

The second decision addresses specific pieces of information that you realize need to be taught as the result of the preassessment. Now you can decide what content you need to reteach or review. Again, you may decide to review content with the whole class or with just a group of learners. In some situations, you will decide to differentiate the learning so that each learner or small groups of learners will be taught the same content.

3. Should I share the preassessment data with the learners and/or their families?

This decision will depend on the unit of learning, the results of the individual preassessment, and the trends that you find from the ongoing preassessments. If you discover that a learner continuously shows extreme strength or weakness and you have consulted with your grade-level colleagues and perhaps the special education team, you want to talk with the learner and the learner's family. The learner or family may tell you that the learner attended a summer math camp or writers' workshop. Likewise, you may discover that the learner was ill and missed a great amount of school near the end of the previous school year, so that much of the previous school year's content was not retained. This question will be one that you confront frequently during your teaching career.

Activities

1. Observe a classroom to try to identify evidence of preassessments.

2. Talk with a classroom teacher about the various kinds of preassessments that the teacher uses to gather baseline data.

3. Look at your favorite learning experience and write one kind of preassessment aligned with the six components of assessment.

4. Describe to another teacher your favorite kind of preassessment that you remember a teacher using in your classroom.

5. Look in a teaching manual to see how the publishers recommend you preassess the learning experiences to document the baseline data.

4

Aligning Appropriate Formative Assessments

As you teach your learning experiences (lesson plans), your mission is to become keenly aware of whether or not your students are engaged. You want to assess how well they are participating in the learning, connecting to prior learning, and understanding the new content and processes. Assessment should occur immediately and frequently, so you can modify and adjust your instruction to ensure that your learners are making steady progress to meet the objectives that guide your learning experience. When you are successful, you see that your learners "get it." You should see this happen several times a day. These moments are some of the most exciting events in your classroom. All of your planning, preparation, and facilitation bring you great joy when you realize that you have effectively fulfilled all six components of assessment.

Every time you check to see whether your learners are "getting it," you are monitoring progress and conducting formative assessments. Formative assessments occur before and during the learning and teaching as your learners comprehend the new knowledge, demonstrate the advanced skills, and acquire the appropriate dispositions along the way. Your formative assessments appraise all types of information that learners exhibit in many different forms.

Consider the Six Components of Assessment

As you collect formative data, you gather, organize, and analyze continuous progress through ongoing feedback and interactions between you and your students to accomplish three goals:

1. To exchange feedback and provide corrections to the learning for the whole class as well as for individual learners; this is formative assessment *as* learning

2. To plan how to modify and adjust the teaching; this is formative assessment *for* learning

3. To amass continuous data to inform and support knowledge, skills, and dispositions so you can note the progress you and your students achieve both during and after the learning and teaching; this is formative assessment *of* learning

Figure 4.1 provides an illustration of your formative assessment goals.

During instruction, you want to check the learning to see if learners are comprehending the content, following your directions,

Figure 4.1 Formative Assessment Goals

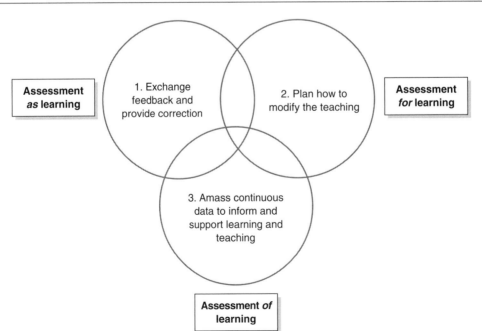

and expressing their learning in ways that are both developmentally appropriate and individually creative. You check the learning through your refined questioning skills that build upon prior knowledge and experiences to increase thinking and connections.

Let's revisit the six components of assessment (refer to Figure 1.1 in Chapter 1). Ask yourself the questions in Table 4.1 to guide you as you start to plan and develop your formative assessments to check the learning and provide feedback to your learners and guidance for yourself.

After you conduct your preassessments and before you develop your formative assessments, there are three important keys to your

Table 4.1 Formative Assessment Questions for the Six Components of Assessment

Component of Assessment	Formative Assessment Questions
1. Each learner's individuality and background	a. What are the cultural characteristics of each student related to a particular unit of learning? b. What are the preferred learning styles of each student related to a particular academic subject area? c. What are the personal interests of each student related to particular content topics and issues?
2. Learner's prior knowledge and experiences	a. What does each student know, do, and believe related to the goals and objectives for a particular unit of learning? b. What does each student want to learn related to a particular unit of learning? c. How does each student prefer to engage in the learning and express new learning?
3. Teacher's expertise and expectations	a. What is your expertise related to the content and processes in a particular academic subject area? Do you have a favorite area or a special interest or skill? Do you have unique experiences to enhance and enrich the learning? b. What knowledge, skills, and dispositions do you want to be sure to teach during the particular unit of learning? c. What knowledge, skills, and dispositions do you want to be sure to integrate across the curriculum and to make connections outside of the classroom for a particular unit of learning?
4. Teacher's organization and readiness	a. What do you know about the unit of learning? b. How do you want to facilitate the learning? What method do you prefer for teaching this subject area? c. What resources can you access to expand your expertise and readiness for this particular unit of learning?

(Continued)

Table 4.1   (Continued)

Component of Assessment	Formative Assessment Questions
5. Curricular content and academic standards	a. How might you connect the student learning expectations with each individual student's prior learning? b. How can you ensure that the learning is student centered, student directed, engaging and providing them with multiple ways to express their learning and exchange ideas? c. How might you make the learning meaningful and relevant?
6. Learning community context	a. How will you reinforce the established community of learners in your classroom to connect with the unit of learning? b. How might you connect learning expectations with the unit of learning? c. How might you connect student learning with the world?

success you should know. The first key is to *design your curriculum* by starting with the end result; the second key is to *align your assessments* with your curriculum and instruction; the third key is to *assign instruction and activities* that enrich the learning. Essential to all three keys is providing your students voice, choice, and ownership or agency in their own learning. This means that you want to create learning environments in which your students (1) are encouraged to share their outcomes as well as their opinions related to learning, (2) are provided opportunities to generate options and select the way they express their own learning, and (3) are invited into the teaching/learning process to personalize the learning and be an equal member in the learning environment. Giving students voice, choice, and ownership or agency will help increase individual responsibility for learning. The first two keys are detailed through the rest of this chapter; the third key awaits you in Chapter 5. These three keys will open the doors to your success with formative assessments.

Design Your Curriculum

The first significant key is to design your curriculum. In middle-level and secondary school classrooms, you are responsible for designing your curriculum for various subject areas and organizing it for each day. Your task is to coordinate the learning and to guide the students so each day is balanced. You want to be aware of the sequence and the difficulty of the learning activities for each subject area so that each day flows smoothly and comfortably for your community of learners . . . and for you.

Most middle-level and secondary school teachers have the benefit of teaching one group of learners throughout the entire year. You can plan your learning experiences and units of learning so that you can plan group outcomes and challenge your students appropriately as the activities compliment one another logically. As you design your curriculum, you can incorporate special events at school and in the community so that the learning, teaching, and schooling are natural, authentic, and holistic.

Here is a list of recommended steps for designing your curriculum:

1. Make a blank copy of the school year calendar to use for planning each of your subject areas.

2. Pencil in all of the days and times dedicated to nonteaching activities, such as assemblies, special events, parent conferences, and so forth.

3. Pencil in all of the deadlines, including holidays, end of the quarters, distribution of grades, and so forth.

4. With the teaching days in front of you, record the daily schedule and the amount of time suggested or prescribed for each subject area. Include any times your students are out of the classroom for anticipated reasons.

5. Focus on one subject area or class period at a time. Look at all the learning expectations that you should cover for one subject area. Group them together into cohesive units of learning. Be sure you check your school's curriculum guide and established syllabi to add anything required in addition to the state standards. This is one of the most vital steps for making your learning student centered and meaningful. Some schools have written guides to help you with this step. Or, if you work on a team, you might complete this step with a colleague. Consider whether you have to coordinate with another subject area and colleague(s) too.

6. Look at all of your units of learning. Place them into a reasonable sequence so you can build the learning from one unit to the next unit. Sequencing the learning applies to both the concepts and practices that you want to establish in your community of learners. For example, after you teach cooperative learning skills, you can use them throughout the year.

7. In order to teach all of your units during the year, you have to allocate the appropriate amount of time to cover all of them

with depth and breadth, and to provide multiple opportunities for learning and expressing the learning.

8. Highlight each unit of learning with a special project to keep the learning engaging and interesting. As you plan, think about the sequence you follow to introduce content and assign activities in relationship to your students' energies. You want to establish a regular routine so you and your students feel comfortable and can anticipate events. However, you want to avoid falling into a predictable rut.

9. Now you can coordinate all of your units of learning so each day flows together smoothly. You may discover that there are times you can combine content and processes from one subject area with another subject area. Or you may realize that you want to change the order of your units in one subject area to complement the order of units in another subject area. The big idea is to draw your blueprints for the entire year for each of your classes. To save yourself energy and angst, be sure that you have spaced out the due dates for your students' major projects so you are not assessing all of them in one night or over one weekend.

10. Stay flexible. Your plans will change and many times. As you conduct your formative assessments, you will modify and adjust your plans frequently. And be sure that you keep all of your notes so you can use them again in the future.

Table 4.2 presents a quick recap of the 10 recommended steps for designing curriculum.

Table 4.2   10 Recommended Steps for Designing Curriculum

1. Make blank copies of the calendar for the school year with one copy for each subject area that you teach.

2. Record all of the nonteaching activities outside of your classroom time.

3. Record all deadlines, grading periods, conferences, and so forth.

4. Make a copy of the suggested or prescribed teaching times for each subject area and the times your learners are out of your classroom.

5. Keep lists of the grade-level curricular standards and student learning expectations for each subject area that you teach. Group the student learning expectations so they form units of learning both within an academic discipline and across academic disciplines.

6. Sequence your units of learning through the school year so you build upon prior understandings, introduce and develop new understandings, then master and advance understandings in an order that fits with the learners and the calendar.

7. Allocate appropriate amounts of time throughout the year for depth, breadth, and multiple opportunities for expressing the learning.

8. Highlight each unit of learning with a special project to keep learning engaging and interesting.

9. Coordinate all units of learning so the day flows together smoothly.

10. Stay flexible so you can make changes as needed and wanted.

Start With the End Result

As you design your curriculum, visualize what you want your students to know, do, and believe at the end of the learning experience. What students *know* refers to concepts or ideas supported by a wide range of information. Concepts involve knowledge, thinking, and thinking about thinking. What students *do* refers to skills. Skills require thinking and applying the concepts to actions. What students *believe* refers to dispositions or outlooks. Dispositions help students to develop characteristics that stimulate creativity, problem solving, decision making, and confidence building. Teachers need to balance the desired concepts, skills, and dispositions comprising the outcomes or end result when designing curriculum and aligning assessments.

Three tables are presented to assist you. Table 4.3 offers a list of thinking concepts with descriptions. Thinking concepts help you identify the types of mental activities that should be involved with understanding concepts in various contexts and situations.

Table 4.3   Thinking Concepts With Descriptions

Concept	Descriptions
Conditional information	Information about the appropriate use of an action or process important to a task
Core thinking	Cognitive operations used in thinking processes

(Continued)

Table 4.3 (Continued)

Critical thinking	Reasonable, reflective thinking that is focused on deciding what to believe, say, or do; awareness of own biases, objectivity, and logic; specific dispositions and skills such as analyzing arguments, seeing other points of view, and reaching sound conclusions
Creative thinking	Ability to form new combinations of ideas to fulfill a need, or to get original or otherwise appropriate results
Declarative information	Factual information
Metacognition	Awareness and control of one's thinking, including commitment, attitudes, and attention
Philosophic tradition	An approach to studying thinking that focuses on broad issues about the nature and quality of thinking and its role in human behavior
Process	Relatively complex sequence of thinking skills
Procedural information	Information about the various actions or processes important to a task
Schemata	Knowledge structures associated with a specific state, event, or concept
Thinking	Process of creating a structured series of connective transactions between items of perceived information; relatively complex and time-consuming cognitive operations, such as concept formation, problem solving, and composing, all of which employ one or more core thinking skills

Activate Your Students' Thinking

Table 4.4 presents a list of thinking skills with descriptions. Once you have identified the concepts to include in your unit of learning or learning experience, reference this list for strategies to involve your students in the learning.

Table 4.4 Thinking Skills With Descriptions

Thinking Skill	Descriptions
Activating prior knowledge	Recalling something learned previously relative to the topic or task
Analyzing	Core thinking skills that involve clarifying information by examining parts and relationships
Attention	Conscious control of mental focus on particular information
Classifying	Grouping entities on the basis of their common attributes
Commitment	An aspect of knowledge and control of self that involves a decision to employ personal energy and resources to control a situation
Comparing	Noting similarities and differences between or among entities
Composing	The process of developing a composition, which may be written, musical, mechanical, or artistic
Comprehending	Generating meaning or understanding by relating new information to prior knowledge
Concept formation	Organizing information about an entity and associating the information with a label (word)
Decision making	Selecting from among alternatives
Defining problems	Focusing and clarifying puzzling situations
Elaborating	Adding details, explanations, examples, or other relevant information from prior knowledge
Encoding	Remembering skills that involve storing information in long-term memory
Establishing criteria	Setting standards for making judgments
Evaluating	Core thinking skills that involve assessing the reasonableness and quality of ideas
Executive control	Evaluating, planning, and regulating the declarative, procedural, and conditional information involved in a task

(Continued)

Table 4.4 (Continued)

Thinking Skill	Descriptions
Focusing	Core thinking skills that involve attention to selected pieces of information and ignoring others
Formulating questions	An information-gathering skill that involves seeking new information through inquiry
Generating	Core thinking skills that involve producing new information, meaning, or ideas
Identifying attributes/ components	Determining characteristics or parts of something
Identifying errors	Disconfirming or proving the falsehood of statements
Identifying relationships/ patterns	Recognizing ways elements are related
Inferring	Going beyond available information to identify what may reasonably be true
Information gathering	Core thinking skills that involve bringing to consciousness the relevant data needed for cognitive processing
Integrating	Core skills that involve connecting or combining information
Knowledge and control of process	A component of metacognition that involves executive control of declarative, procedural, and conditional information relative to a task
Mnemonics	A set of encoding strategies that involve linking bits of information together through visual or semantic connections
Observing	An information-gathering skill that involves obtaining information through one or more senses
Oral discourse	Talking with other people
Ordering	Sequencing entities according to a given criterion
Organizing	Core thinking skills that involve arranging information so that it can be used more effectively
Planning	Developing strategies to reach a specific goal; delineation of end-means relationships

Thinking Skill	Descriptions
Predicting	Anticipating an outcome based on the use of one's personal knowledge
Principle formation	Recognizing a relationship between or among concepts
Problem solving	Analyzing a perplexing or difficult situation for the purpose of generating a solution
Recalling	Remembering skills that involve retrieving information from long-term memory
Regulating	Checking one's progress toward a goal
Rehearsal	An encoding strategy that involves repeated processing of information
Remembering	Core thinking skills that involve conscious efforts to store and retrieve information
Representing	Changing the form of information to show how critical elements are related
Research	Conducting inquiry for the purpose of confirming or validating one or more hypotheses
Restructuring	Changing existing knowledge structures to incorporate new information
Retrieval	Accessing previously encoded information
Self-knowledge and self-control	A component of metacognition that involves commitment, attitudes, and attention
Setting goals	A focusing skill that involves establishing direction and purpose
Summarizing	Combining information efficiently into a cohesive statement
Verifying	Confirming the accuracy, truth, or quality of an observation, hypothesis, claim, or product

Select Optimal Teaching Techniques

Table 4.5 presents a list of thinking processes with descriptions. From this list you can select teaching techniques for advancing the skills and understand the concepts.

Table 4.5   Thinking Processes With Descriptions

Core Process	Descriptions
Analyzing	• Clarifying existing information by examining parts and relationships • Identifying attributes and components: determining characteristics or the parts of something • Identifying relationships and patterns: recognizing ways elements are related • Identifying main ideas: identifying the central element; for example, the hierarchy of key ideas in a message or line of reasoning • Identifying errors: recognizing logical fallacies and other mistakes and, where possible, correcting them
Evaluating	• Assessing the reasonableness and quality of ideas • Establishing criteria: setting standards for making judgments • Verifying: confirming the accuracy of claims
Focusing	• Attending to selected pieces of information and ignoring others • Defining problems: clarifying needs, discrepancies, or puzzling situations • Setting goals: establishing direction and purpose
Generating	• Producing new information, meaning, or ideas • Inferring: going beyond available information to identify what may reasonably be true • Predicting: anticipating next events, or the outcome of a situation • Elaborating: explaining by adding details, examples, or other relevant information
Information gathering	• Bringing to consciousness the relative data needed for cognitive processing • Observing: obtaining information through one or more senses • Formulating questions: seeing new information through inquiry
Integrating	• Connecting and combining information • Summarizing: combining information efficiently into a cohesive statement • Restructuring: changing existing knowledge structures to incorporate new information

Core Process	Descriptions
Organizing	• Arranging information so it can be used more effectively • Comparing and contrasting: noting similarities and differences between or among entities • Classifying: grouping and labeling entities on the basis of their attribute • Ordering: sequencing entities according to a giver criterion • Representing: changing the form, but not the substance of information
Remembering	• Storing and retrieving information • Encoding: storing information in long-term memory • Recalling: retrieving information from long-term memory

Identify the outcomes and the final products that your learners will produce to document mastery of the content and processes. (Many different summative assessments are provided in Chapter 7.) Your task is to design the instructional activities that you will implement to inform and guide your learners to achieve success on the final, summative assessments.

You will continually check to see whether your learners understand the learning through your formative assessments. It is suggested that you make a detailed list of goals or big ideas that addresses each of the six components of assessment to ensure that your curriculum and instruction are holistic and complete. Your list of goals might look like this for a unit on positive and negative numbers:

1. *Learners:* To describe what positive and negative numbers are; to identify positive and negative numbers on a paper; to explain the meanings of positive and negative numbers

2. *Learning:* To understand the properties and purposes of positive and negative numbers in math and in life

3. *Teacher:* To share the fascination associated with positive and negative numbers

4. *Teaching:* To engage learners in self-discovery and multiple forms of shared expression in ways that are developmentally appropriate

5. *Curriculum:* To fulfill grade-level student learning expectations through isolated learning experiences or integrated units of learning

6. *Community:* To provide an opportunity for learners to recognize positive and negative numbers in the world around them

By starting at the end and working backward, you are mapping the journey from your destination back to the beginning. This approach is called BAM: the Backwards Assessment Model (Wiggins & McTighe, 1998). Design each step of the learning and teaching by matching where you (in conjunction with the state and school district) want the learners to be at the end of the process with the baseline data you gathered during the entry-level preassessments.

For example, during a learning experience related to positive and negative numbers in a seventh-grade math classroom, you could preassess the learners using a written assessment with 10 numbers printed on a page. You read the following directions aloud and demonstrate the appropriate response mechanisms on the board: "Draw a red circle O around each of the positive numbers. Draw a blue square □ around each of the negative numbers." You tell the learners that they will draw a total of five red circles and five blue squares. But it is essential that you do not give your learners hints or assist your learners in any other way. Remember, you want to preassess to reveal their entry-level knowledge, skills, and dispositions. This is the time to observe and to begin some anecdotal records to add to the written preassessment baseline data.

Give your learners a limited amount of time to complete these tasks so they do not struggle too much, become anxious, or grow bored. Reassure your learners that you want to see what they understand about positive and negative numbers at this time. Then collect the papers and move on to a different math learning experience or a learning experience related to another subject. You are urged to administer your preassessments early in the class period or day to reduce any growing concerns and to avoid immediate questions.

Organize Outcomes and Coordinate Levels

As you design your curriculum by starting with the end, you will organize the outcomes. First, you want to organize the outcomes stemming from your curriculum and instruction (Wiggins & McTighe, 1998). You want to organize important outcomes as:

1. Immediate recognition of information (II) that your learners need and want to know now; for example, *Does this word need a capital letter?*

2. Continuing development of essential concepts (CC) and skills that your students need to know and be able to do to advance the learning; for example, *What kinds of words should be capitalized?*

3. Unending lifelong understandings (UU) and wisdom that your learners need to acquire, apply, and appreciate; for example, *Why do we capitalize words? How does capitalization help us?*

You may be able to organize your curricular and instructional outcomes for the entire class, or you may need to differentiate (Tomlinson, 2007/2008) the learning and teaching to small groups or individuals. You cannot make these decisions until you have conducted your preassessments. Then as you gather your baseline or entry-level data, you will be able to organize these outcomes right away.

Gathering preassessment baseline data simultaneously while documenting your anecdotal records also allows you to determine whether the upcoming learning experience should be an *introductory-, developmental-,* or *mastery*-level learning experience to initiate your learning experience or unit of learning. This means that, after reviewing the entry-level data, you ask yourself if the learners need to start in one of six places:

1. At the beginning of the unit to introduce (I) the knowledge, skills, and dispositions

2. With some review of the learning to remediate (R) prior to beginning the unit (you cannot remediate until you have introduced the unit and can review or remediate necessary learning)

3. At the middle of the unit to develop (D) learning

4. During the unit to progress and become proficient (P) with the learning

5. At the close of the unit to master (M) the learning

6. With more complex and integrated applications to advance (A) the learning

Most likely, you will discover that your learners exhibit various levels of understanding, requiring you to organize several different groups of learners, some of whom operate at each level at various times throughout the unit. You will check your students' progress during the entire sequence, including the preassessments, the formative assessments, and summative assessments as shown in Figure 4.2; Figure 4.2 can help you organize your outcomes.

Figure 4.2   Organizing Expectations, Leveling Outcomes, and Collecting
Assessments

Step 1: Designing curriculum and assigning instruction	Immediate Information (II)	Continuous Concepts (CC)	Unending Understanding (UU)

Step 1: For each learning experience and unit of learning, you must decide the immediate information, the continuous concepts, and the unending understanding that you want your students to gain through the knowledge, skills, and dispositions related to a particular subject; your decisions allow you to design the curriculum and assign instruction.

Step 2: Leveling outcomes of learning and teaching	Advanced (A)	Mastery (M)	Proficiency (P)	Developmental (D)	Remedial (R)	Introductory (I)

Step 2: Once the II, CC, and UU are identified, you must decide the specific levels of outcomes you anticipate your learners to demonstrate as a group and as individuals through their assessments. Levels are documented as rubrics, checklists, and percentages.

Step 3: Collecting preassessment, baseline, or entry-level data	Step 4: Collecting formative assessment, or progress-monitoring data	Step 5: Collecting summative assessment, final, or concluding data

Steps 3, 4, and 5: You will guide students through each step for each learning experience and unit of learning leading to evaluation and accountability.

Align Assessments With Curriculum and Instruction

The second significant key to success assessment is to align your baseline and formative performance-based assessments with the curriculum and instruction. In order to map the journey from end to start, first, you identify what the learners will learn—the curriculum—and, second, you describe how the learning and teaching will occur—the instruction.

Continuing with our unit of learning on positive and negative numbers, you decide to divide the class into three groups, one at each level: introductory, developmental, and mastery. Although you are teaching the concepts of positive and negative numbers, each group of learners will be held to a different expectation. Immediately both your curriculum and instruction are modified to match then to the expectation that you will assess along the way. These quick checks are the formative assessments. They inform your practice during the learning experience and help you formulate what to teach at each step of the journey.

Strive for Breadth and Depth

As you align your curriculum and instruction with the assessment, you guarantee that your forms of appraisal along the way and at the end match what you want your learners to learn and how you will engage them in the learning process. For example, as you teach about positive and negative numbers, you decide the breadth of the curriculum; that is, the numbers your seventh grade learners will analyze, such as whole numbers, fractions, and decimals. You also decide the depth of the curriculum; that is, being able to place positive and negative numbers on a number line, to add and subtract positive and negative numbers, and to multiply and divide positive and negative numbers.

Likewise, you determine the breadth of the instruction; that is, the tools or manipulatives you will use to show your learners the concepts and processes for analyzing positive and negative whole number, fractions, and decimals. Then you decide the depth of the instruction; that is, the many different kinds of connections to the students' world you will incorporate into the learning experience to ensure that your learners understand completely. All the while, you provide multiple opportunities for your students to express and exchange their learning with their peers.

You continually check the learning using a variety of forms of appraisal, such as writing, speaking, and demonstration, to be sure that you have aligned the breadth and depth of the curriculum and instruction in ways that are motivating, engaging, and developmentally appropriate. All of your formative assessments become progress-monitoring feedback related to each of the six components of assessment (refer back to Table 4.1). You are monitoring the learners and learning, the teacher and teaching, the curricular content and the community context. All six components continue to operate holistically. When you modify one component, your adjustments influence the other five components.

Develop Your Assessments

Table 4.6 provides guidelines and examples for developing your assessments. The guidelines need to be completed in the same order as they are numbered here.

Table 4.6 Guidelines for Developing Assessments

Guidelines	Examples
1. Identify the focus of the assessment	Change fractions to decimals and decimals to fractions with progressive difficulty
2. Determine source of the assessment, that is, on file, borrowed, modified, or new	Modify and reduce the chapter posttest found in the textbook
3. Place assessment into a learning context, that is, time, place, and purpose	Administer assessment after completing the previous chapter during the regular math class period to determine competence and comfort with functions
4. Detail assessment procedures	Sitting at individual desks, learners will be given a single sheet with approximately 20 math problems to be completed in pencil within 10 minutes
5. Preview instructions for assessing	Learners complete as many problems as possible working silently and independently; learners are encouraged to show any calculations that they use to solve the math problems
6. Prepare the assessment	Referencing the posttest printed in the math textbook, select 20 problems of increasing difficulty: 10 problems changing fractions into decimals, and 10 problems changing decimals into fractions
7. Score the assessment	Complete the pretest to create a scoring guide and use the scoring guide to score the students' papers
8. Analyze effectiveness of the assessment	Record the preassessment data and determine where the learning should begin for each learner or for groups of learners and whether the assessment aligns with the curriculum and instruction; disaggregate the data through an item analysis to identify needs and priorities
9. Plan for instruction	Determine the amount of time predicted for mastering the learning; collect resources and materials; collaborate with colleagues; schedule the unit of learning
10. Conduct formative assessments	Conduct formative assessments to collect progress-monitoring data as the unit unfolds; compare and contrast formative data with preassessment data to note progress

Explore Cognition Via Patterns of Thought

Monitoring your students' progress with formative assessments presents ideal opportunities to enhance your students' thinking. You want your students to think using three different patterns of thought (Garner, 2007):

1. *Comparative thinking:* How people, places, and things are alike and different. Patterns of comparative thinking include recognition and recall (memorization); classification; spatial orientation; temporal orientation; conservation of constancies; and metaphorical thinking.

2. *Symbolic representation:* Culturally acceptable coding systems that translate thoughts into conversations, actions, and interactions. Patterns of symbolic representation are verbal and nonverbal, such as math, music, and rhythm; movements, dance, and gestures; interpersonal interactions; graphics such as drawings, paintings, and logos.

3. *Logical reasoning:* Abstract thinking. Patterns of logical reasoning include deductive and inductive reasoning; analogical and hypothetical thinking; cause-effect relationships; analysis, synthesis, and evaluation; problem framing and problem solving.

Every learner develops unique internalization and manifestations of cognition using individual patterns of thought. Yet, as we all continue to learn throughout life, the three patterns of thought can be introduced and developed at all ages and stages, especially when learners make valuable connections to prior learning, current purposes, and their personal lives.

Promote Deductive and Inductive Thinking

You also want to include questions that promote deductive and inductive thinking. *Deductive thinking* starts with the general idea and moves to the specific. For example, if you are studying climate and weather, you could ask a deductive question asking for types of weather patterns. Deductive thinking generates details.

Inductive thinking starts with the specifics and moves to the general idea. You could ask an inductive question asking learners to describe today's weather and draw the inference that the conditions are just right for a thunderstorm later in the day. Inductive thinking generates ideas.

Some of your learners prefer to start with the general idea and use deductive thinking to supply the examples. You may recognize that this is the way you usually teach too. You state that the class will be studying the food groups and then you identify the groups and examples of each group. It might be helpful for you to remember deductive thinking as you deliver the whole and dissect into the parts. You may want learners to use deductive thinking to itemize a prescribed set of subsets or examples to illustrate the concept, topic, or issue. However, deductive thinking may be more closed and restricting.

Some learners and teachers prefer to start with inductive thinking. Many different examples are given on a subject and then the overall idea or issue. It might be helpful for you to remember inductive thinking as introducing the parts to lead to the whole. Inductive thinking tends to be more open ended and exploratory in nature. You and your learners can investigate and come to conclusions or big ideas collaboratively.

Consider Sequential and Spatial Thinking

Patterns of thought occur in two ways: sequentially and spatially. Sequential thinking means looking at the world and attending to tasks in a step-by-step, linear fashion. Some students and some teachers prefer to operate this way. Thinking and acting sequentially involves organization of information, linear deductive reasoning, singular analysis, and gradual progression from simple to complex. Sequence is influenced by auditory senses, especially language, and an awareness of time.

Spatial thinking means looking at the world through an intuitive grasp of complex systems and a synthesis of multiple stimuli simultaneously. Spatial thinking involves inductive thinking and a generation of new, creative, imaginary ideas, often skipping steps by combining existing facts into different ways. Spatial thinking is influenced by visual senses and an awareness of space.

It is helpful when teachers realize whether their teaching tends to favor sequential or spatial thinking and how they ask questions of their learners. Likewise, teachers need to preassess their learners early in the school year to know which students are sequential learners and which ones are spatial learners. Some students may exhibit a refined balance of both sequential and spatial learning, while other students would benefit from additional experiences with both techniques. Teachers' questioning skills can enhance learners' competence and confidence with each skill.

Remember Divergent and Convergent Thinking

Another set of critical questions that enhance cognition includes divergent and convergent thinking. With *divergent thinking,* learners offer all kinds of creative responses. Divergent thinking tends to be open ended and associated with problem solving. Divergent thinking is similar to deductive thinking in that many different details are supplied.

Conversely, with *convergent thinking,* the examples are leading to one big idea. The learning converges or meets at one place. This is similar to inductive thinking in that you are leading to one big issue.

Plan With Competence and Confidence . . .

Formative assessments provide you with the best guidance to ensure that your curriculum and instruction are planned efficiently and facilitated effectively. As you implement performance-based formative assessments more frequently, you will gain in competence and confidence. You will be able to provide for your learners' needs and expand your instruction in new directions.

From a teacher:

The biggest change I have made in my teaching during my 10 years in the classroom is understanding and using formative assessments. I watch, listen, and learn about my learners and my teaching every day as I conduct the formative assessments. The learners tell me exactly what I need to do next. Now my classroom is all about them (and not me).

Extend With Questions and Activities

Frequently Asked Questions

1. Should I keep a list of the performance-based assessments I use for every unit of learning?

It is strongly recommend that you do this. You will be amazed at how quickly and easily organizing a system will become for you with time and practice. You will know which assessments you use most frequently, which ones are most effective, which ones are least effective, which ones you are avoiding, and so forth. You simply cannot evaluate what you are doing until you have the data or evidence to review. Plus—and this is the bonus—once you have developed your performance-based assessments for your units of learning, you merely have to adjust them the next time. You won't believe how much they will save your planning time in the future. (And your school administrators will be extremely impressed with your professionalism.)

2. What is the best way to store and access my records?

You want to keep a copy on your computer and make a hard copy to keep with your plans. Make backup computer copies and use technological devices that you can carry to school with you to use during your planning periods. You might want to make multiple hard copies, too, so you can keep an original in your files, one to check off as you complete the assessment and make notes for effectiveness, and one to record necessary future revisions. Although computers are a fantastic improvement for teachers, many thoughts will pop into your mind at times when you cannot access a computer immediately.

3. Should I share my records with my learners and/or their families?

You might want to show your learners and their families your system to illustrate how you align curriculum and instruction planned specifically for your learners. Most likely they will be quite impressed.

Activities

1. Using one of your learning experiences, select a common manipulative for your learners to demonstrate a formative assessment to you.

2. Write three different formative performance-based assessments you can use for a favorite unit of learning.

3. Show your learners how you want them to demonstrate their learning to you at the end of the first learning experience in a unit of learning.

4. Tell a colleague about a success formative assessment that you implement in your classroom regularly.

5. Start a record-keeping system to become aware of your current methods for conducting formative assessments in your classroom.

5

Incorporating Learning, Assigning Instruction Followed by Feedback and Correction

Formative assessments are extremely important and are conducted throughout the school year, so let's review briefly. In Chapter 4, you were introduced to the first two keys to your success in the classroom: one, *design the curriculum* to be standards based, learner centered, and data driven; and, two, *align the assessments* with the curriculum and instruction so students are given choice, voice, and ownership. You have conducted your preassessments collecting baseline or entry-level data, determined goals for you and your learners (both collectively and individually), and are ready to begin conducting formative assessments *for* learning, *as* learning, and *of* learning as you implement the third key: *Assign your instruction and activities.*

Instruction that is engaging, efficient, and effective requires that teachers incorporate valuable pedagogical strategies that produce formative assessment data to inform and support the learning and teaching. You want to (1) feature and integrate a variety of practical learning experiences, (2) seek and give useful feedback, and (3) reinforce and redirect learners' progress with appropriate correction in the classroom.

Assign Your Instruction and Activities

The third key to your success is to assign your instruction and activities with a selection of practical instructional strategies that will empower you to modify the ways that you teach and the ways that your students demonstrate their outcomes. Through your formative assessments, you can monitor students' progress toward understanding using assorted strategies, checking the acquisition and application of both immediate information (II) and continuous concepts (CC). The seven approaches include learning that is scaffolded, spiral, compacted, integrated, project based, holistic, and constructivist. You can incorporate these seven approaches independently or in combination with one another. And each instructional approach offers a unique strategy for conducting formative assessments.

Scaffold the Learning

To *scaffold* the learning means to build upon students' prior knowledge and experiences. You can scaffold in two different ways. One way is to construct the new learning upon prior learning from past years, earlier in the same school year during another learning experience or unit, or from the previous few days within the current unit of learning. The second way is to scaffold by providing additional information and support for specific parts of the developing concepts and practices that challenge the whole class or individual learners during the new instruction. You continually check to see if your learners are engaged and have solidified their understanding through formative assessments. When you scaffold the learning successfully, you connect the end result with your beginning goal while aligning the formative assessments with your curriculum and instruction.

Imagine some scaffolding assembled next to a structure under construction. The new building represents the assessment. The architect has drawn the blueprints of the structure illustrating the end product. The blueprints represent the curriculum. The engineer has identified the planned sequence of steps, the materials that will be needed at each step, and the tools that are necessary at each step to construct the structure. The plan represents the instruction. As the structure grows in size, the scaffolding grows next to it so the builders can reach the structure efficiently and complete their tasks successfully. Or the scaffolding can be used to attend to specific challenges that need special attention encountered along the way.

The learning experience also could be one that revisits or builds on prior learning. When you build on prior learning, you scaffold to introduce, advance, or construct new learning based on past accomplishments. For example, imagine that you are teaching adverbs to your eighth grade language arts class. You show your learners a sentence and identify the nouns, verbs, and adjectives, reminding learners about relationships between nouns and adjectives and how adjectives describe nouns:

> Suddenly, nine of the closest green stems brilliantly bloomed into huge yellow sunflowers.

Then you ask your learners to identify the words that end with *-ly* and describe verbs. You are scaffolding or *building the learning upon prior learning* as you introduce adverbs.

This is exactly how scaffolding occurs in your classroom. You draw the blueprint as you develop your curriculum; you design a plan, identify the materials, supply the tools, manage the project, and continue to assemble the scaffold so each learner can reach the structure and complete the task. Your scaffolding will be effective based on the data collected from your formative assessments. You will know exactly what to teach and how to teach it by monitoring the progress throughout the entire teaching/learning process.

Here is an illustration using an example to help you remember how to scaffold:

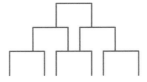

The prior knowledge and experiences establish the first tier or foundation; you introduce the second tier with new content and processes. Then you conduct your formative assessments at the third level as you check the learning. You continue to scaffold as you teach and assess. Formative assessments may occur any time during the learning experience or unit to provide immediate feedback to you and your students.

Spiral Prior Learning

You can *spiral* the learning. That means you revisit prior learning and incorporate it into the new learning as you introduce or construct new learning. Using our previous learning with adverbs, you spiral the learning as you modify the uses of the adjectives. For example, after your students have identified the adverbs in several sample sentences as a whole class, in small groups, or individually, you look at the same sentences to find examples of adverbs that indicate time, place, cause, or degree to answer questions such as "How?" "When?" "Where?" "How much?" or "How many?"

Suddenly, nine of the closest green stems brilliantly bloomed into huge yellow sunflowers.

Through spiral learning, first, you prepare your learners through planning and introduction; second, you help them to construct new knowledge through practice and development; and finally, you guide your learners to reflect upon the new discoveries and place them into a personal context through meaningful connections to the world around them. All the while you conduct formative assessments to check the learning of the new concepts and practices. Here is an illustration to help you visualize the process of spiral learning:

Compact Learning Logically

A third approach to organizing the instruction is to *compact* the learning. That means you compress and condense as much meaningful learning into one learning experience as is possible and productive. Visualize a box into which you are packing clothing. You continue to shove as much into the box as the box can hold and you can lift.

This is what you are doing when you compact the learning. Again, you can see the importance for conducting formative assessments as you compress and condense the learning. Once your learners "get it," you can move onto new concepts and practices. Too many teachers tend to overteach information and applications that their learners have already conquered and spend too little time teaching new concepts and practices. You can easily recognize how you can cover much more of your curriculum by conducting frequent formative assessments. Here is an illustration to help you visualize compact learning:

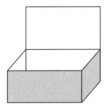

Integrate Learning Across the Curriculum

When you *integrate* the curriculum, you combine two or more student learning expectations into a single learning experience or a single unit of learning. It is essential that you are attentive to the formative assessments when you integrate so that you are sure what your students have learned. It is easy to assess the learning and falsely presume that your learners have conquered all of the student learning expectations when you actually assessed only one or some of the integrated outcomes and you do not know whether your learners mastered all of the learning expectations.

Integrated curriculum can be multidisciplinary in that the curriculum combines several learner learning expectations from within the same academic discipline. Many middle-level and some secondary school teachers use multidisciplinary integration. Perhaps one student learning expectation addresses continents and one addresses oceans. Many teachers would integrate the two expectations when teaching world geography. The key is to conduct formative assessments that check the learning related to each student learning expectation.

Integrated curriculum can be interdisciplinary in that the curriculum combines several student learning expectations from different academic disciplines. More middle-level and secondary school teachers use this approach as they grow in their practice. For example, you might combine teaching about continents and oceans from the social studies curriculum with a piece of literature from the reading curriculum. Now when you are conducting your formative assessments, you must be more careful that you are assessing each student learning expectation.

Here are the illustrations to help you remember this instructional approach:

Multidisciplinary Integrated
Curriculum

Interdisciplinary Integrated
Curriculum

Offer Project-Based Learning

Project-based learning encompasses an approach that expands upon the typical one-class-period teacher-centered learning experiences by shifting the learning to longer, integrated, student-centered projects through which students examine real-world issues. Learners are provided voice, choice, and ownership or agency by designing their own investigations, selecting their own study teams, formulating their own inquiries, seeking information through multiple sources, and developing their own answers that they share with other learners and various other audiences. The three main features of project-based learning are (1) the projects are authentic, (2) the learners take initiative, and (3) each team tackles a different project so that everyone learns from everyone else. This approach greatly increases the learning and lets students teach one another. The projects are performance-based assessments.

Students control the parameters of the project, the schedule, and the presentations. Teachers become coaches and co-learners while maintaining control of the overall progress. Many middle-level and secondary school students reveal that anything close to project-based learning establishes their most satisfying and rewarding moments in school.

Project-based learning requires teachers to conduct formative assessments frequently and in various ways to guarantee that learners are making appropriate progress. Students and teachers can design the formative assessments together; then students can self-assess and conference with the teacher while the teacher provides feedback and documents progress.

Explore Holistic Learning

Holistic learning is an approach to instruction that features learning that is purposeful, natural, and authentic. You link together learning expectations across the curriculum that establish constructs or the major foundations of conceptual or global understanding. You link expectations as webs with connections to all four domains of learning: cognitive, psychomotor, affective, and psychosocial (see Chapter 2). As you explore holistic learning with your students, it is helpful to visualize the constructs that go into building the concept as a metaphor or analogy.

For example, the concept of social justice is built from many different constructs, each with assorted meanings to your learners. Every teacher strives to include social justice as a concept and a practice. You can use inductive or deductive thinking as you design a learning experience, building the constructs that support the concept of social justice. Ultimately, you want your students to visualize the outcomes, create metaphors, and explore possible outcomes that each student can accept and adopt.

A student might visualize social justice as listening to one another through the metaphor of a giant ear. Then the student brainstorms possible outcomes that feature thinking, doing, believing, and interacting so the learning is holistic, such as giant ears on a lightbulb.

The formative assessment is conducted as you watch, listen, read, interact, and reflect throughout the acquisition, application, and appreciation of the learning. Holistic learning is an approach that promotes the benefits of higher-order thinking and the realities of life-long learning.

Try Constructivist Learning

The seventh approach that promotes formative assessments focuses on the *constructivist* philosophy of learning. Constructivism encourages students to plunge into the learning and be creative to achieve the expectations. Using this philosophy requires teachers to allow for learner autonomy and initiative. You design learning experiences or units of learning through which students can express their learning individually and independently using the tools and techniques that fit. As the students and teachers process ideas and produce outcomes, teachers challenge thinking using higher-order questions (see Chapter 4). Teachers must be prepared for unintended consequences, as the curriculum may follow an unanticipated path that, ultimately, becomes more worthy and worthwhile that learners share with one another. Sharing with and teaching one's peers far outweigh reporting to the teacher for stimulating curiosity and inquiry.

Although classrooms following the constructivist philosophy generate and allow for more freedom and creativity, they are not chaotic and uncontrolled. You can easily maintain a well-managed, democratic classroom that supports constructivist learning and assessments.

From a teacher:

We read the book, To Kill a Mockingbird, *by Harper Lee, to start a unit about race in the United States. I asked the learners to collect an oral history from a family member, friend, or neighbor to class on Friday. I was astonished at the stories that the learners shared. Immediately I recognized the importance of expanding the unit. The next week I opened the conversation allowing learners to design their own expressions about equity that they could construct individually, with partners, or as a small group. Everyone had to conference with me to talk about the design; at that time I asked some key questions to prompt their thinking. A week later, learners shared their products. It was phenomenal what everyone learned through the process. We repeated this constructivist approach several times throughout the year. The parents told me these were the times when their children liked school the most.*

Like holistic learning, formative assessments occur during constructivist learning through watching, listening, reading, interacting, and reflecting to the acquisition, application, and appreciation of the processes, products, and people.

Table 5.1 summarizes teaching/learning approaches and provides examples of formative assessments.

Employ Multiple Instructional Strategies

In addition to the seven approaches to learning, it is imperative that you consider Marzano's (2000) nine research-based instructional strategies that increase a classroom teacher's effectiveness and learners' achievement levels. Each of these nine strategies leads to learning techniques that provide formative assessment data:

1. *Similarities and differences.* Teachers guide learners in comparing and contrasting; clarifying; using metaphors and analogies.

2. *Summarizing and note taking.* Teachers guide learners in deconstructing and analyzing information for understanding the content.

3. *Reinforcement and recognition.* Teachers emphasize learners' efforts to meet challenges and achieve.

Table 5.1   Teaching/Learning Approaches and Formative Assessments

Teaching/Learning	Examples of Formative Assessments
1. Scaffolded learning	• What did you learn yesterday in Chapter 1? • Let's think back to the first step in solving this kind of math problem to build on our learning.
2. Spiral learning	• Here you see another blue line on the map. What does it represent? • What kind of punctuation do you need to place at the end of this sentence?
3. Compacted learning	• After you read the list of federal government's nutritional expectations, you and your partner will create a menu of the meals for one day.
4. Integrated learning	• Pretend you are traveling in an imaginary time and space. Write a story and draw a picture.
5. Project-based learning	• For this book report, you are going to work with a partner and create an advertisement with the following items.
6. Holistic learning	• In your small groups, brainstorm and record all the ways people in our community could help save electricity and how that will help us.
7. Constructivist learning	• Create two approaches for solving this problem in our classroom.

4. *Homework and practice.* Teachers provide meaningful activities for learners to deepen understanding and to strengthen skills.

5. *Nonlinguistic representations.* Teachers use graphic organizers, physical models, mental pictures, drawings, and kinesthetic classroom manipulatives and activities.

6. *Cooperative learning.* Teachers facilitate learning experience to promote positive interdependence; face-to-face interactions; individual and group accountability; interpersonal and small group skills; and group processing.

7. *Goal setting and feedback.* Teachers establish a direction for learning that incorporates opportunities through which students can be accountable for their own learning.

8. *Hypotheses generation and testing.* Teachers guide learners in systems analyses, inventions, inquiry, experimentation, decision making, and problem solving.

9. *Prior learning activation.* Teachers use cues, questions, and advance organizers to preview the learning experiences and build upon prior learning (accomplished when you scaffold, spiral, compact, and integrate the learning).

Table 5.2 presents Marzano's nine instructional strategies with examples of formative assessments.

Table 5.2   Marzano's Instructional Strategies With Formative Assessments

Instructional Strategy	*Examples of Formative Assessments*
1. Similarities and differences	• What do these five items have in common? • How are these two items different?
2. Summarizing and note taking	• What was a main idea of the speaker's talk? • Record the time that each event occurs.
3. Reinforcement and recognition	• I like the way you wrote your paragraph. • Let's all show our appreciation for his help.
4. Homework and practice	• For homework, you are to read your poems to a family member. • For practice, you are to write a thank-you note to the school principal.
5. Nonlinguistic representations	• What does this symbol represent to most people in the United States? • Why is this symbol used? What might be another symbol that could be used?
6. Cooperative learning	• Share your lists of favorite foods in your small groups, and decide which items to include in your healthy habits poster.
7. Goal setting and feedback	• Write one goal you have for the new year. • Let me show you how to divide that number into thirds.
8. Hypotheses generation and testing	• What do you think is going to happen, and why do you think as you do? • How can you check your thinking?
9. Prior learning activation	• What did you learn about reading maps? • What is one place you would like to visit?

Consider These Assessment Recommendations

Here are some recommendations for conducting performance-based formative assessments throughout all of the instructional approaches, philosophies, and strategies:

1. Administer formative assessments frequently.

2. Conduct formative assessments close to the new learning.

3. Create shorter assessments; they are better than longer ones.

4. Use forms of appraisal that match the instructional practice.

5. Assess each objective separately so you are sure what you are assessing.

6. Consider the depth, breadth, and opportunities associated with your questions and discussions.

7. Be equitable in the distribution of your questions by race/ethnicity, gender, socioeconomic status, English language learning, special education needs, and so forth.

8. Allow adequate reflection and response time.

9. Provide feedback and reinforcement frequently.

10. Insert correction and redirection as needed.

A list of additional formative assessments is shown in Table 5.3.

Table 5.3   Formative Assessment Ideas

Formative Assessment Ideas	Descriptions
Artwork	• Illustrate a person, place, or thing in artwork • Use a variety of media
Cartoons	• Create a cartoon • Analyze a cartoon
Collections	• Share a collection • Describe a collection
Conversations	• Participate in a conversation • Analyze a conversation

(Continued)

Table 5.3 (Continued)

Formative Assessment Ideas	Descriptions
Dances	• Participate in a dance • Create a dance
Designs	• Create an artistic or architectural design • Create an academic or time related design
Drawings	• Create a drawing • Analyze a drawing
Documentaries	• Describe a documentary • Analyze a documentary
Experiments	• Plan an experiment • Conduct an experiment
Foreign language exchanges	• Participate in a foreign language exchange • Analyze dynamics associated with foreign language exchanges
Games	• Play a game • Create a game for a specific reason
Journals	• Write in a journal • Give reasons for writing in a journal
Letters	• Write a letter • Respond to a letter
Maps	• Read a map • Draw a map
Models	• Create a model of an operation • Analyze the model of an operation
Music: performed	• Perform music • Analyze music
Music: written	• Read music • Write music
Notebooks	• Organize a notebook • Share a completed notebook
Performances	• Create a performance • Deliver a performance
Plays	• Participate in a play • Write a play

Formative Assessment Ideas	Descriptions
Reports	• Write a report • Share a report
Stories	• Write a story • Analyze a story
Worksheets	• Complete a worksheet • Analyze the purposes of a worksheet

Include All Kinds of Questions With Your Formative Assessments

Developing formative assessments involves asking questions and promoting critical thinking with your students. Through the types and techniques guiding your questioning, you can enhance understanding and establish productive ways of thinking.

Asking questions is one of the most effective and efficient ways to check to see if your learners "get it," so you can monitor and adjust their progress immediately and frequently during formative assessments. What you ask and how you ask it can capture your students' attention, challenge their thinking, pique their curiosity, and reinforce the main ideas. You can engage students in the learning, diagnose concerns, start an investigation, and delve into their rationale. Plus you can maintain the pace, guide the conversation, encourage exchange of ideas among learners, and reinforce their efforts.

You can help your learners predict outcomes, make hypotheses, look for answers while reading, anticipate events, follow steps, and comprehend conclusions. You can increase thinking skills with open and closed questions, inductive and deductive thinking, convergent and divergent thinking (see Chapter 4). You can enhance your learners' levels of achievement and enjoyment when they can read their textbooks and subject matter with confidence and competence. Perhaps you want to use word cards or charts with the words *Who, What, Where, How, When,* and *Why* posted on them to prompt your learners to look and listen for information as they are reading a passage, listening to a discussion, and/or watching a video.

Your learners will also learn to watch for obvious and hidden clues, find similarities and differences, make direct and indirect connections, and think creatively. Refining your expertise in the types of questions you ask and the forms of questioning you use will make all the difference for your learners in both what they learn and how they learn. You can change the depth, breadth, and opportunities informing and supporting your learners' knowledge, skills, and dispositions through your refined questioning skills. Plus, you are asking questions not only to conduct your formative assessments. You are modeling how to ask questions so your learners will acquire this expertise for themselves.

Pose Powerful Questions

Powerful questions can be grouped into four main categories. The four categories with subsets and starters include:

I. *Information Questions.* Direct information questions are useful for starting a discussion, establishing the facts related to the topic or issue, and including students who might not be as knowledgeable or comfortable.

   1. *Knowledge:* "Who?" "What?" "Where?" "How?" "When?" "Why?"

   2. *Precision:* "What is an example?" "How much does that make?" "What is the final result?"

   3. *Prompting:* "What is another example?" "Why not?" "How could you solve that problem a different way?"

   4. *Reflective:* "How can you summarize your thoughts?" "How else can you say that?" "How did you feel about that?"

II. *Probing Questions.* Probing questions advance thinking and understanding by establishing relationships establishing what something is and what it is not. Probing questions help to expand class discussions.

   1. *Clarifying:* "How can you make that idea clearer for us?" "Why do you think that happened?" "How do you think the people felt?"

   2. *Understanding:* "How would you explain the situation to someone else?" "What should that person have said?" "What is a different outcome?"

   3. *Offering ideas and insights:* "What is another way of presenting that information?" "What do you think made that happen?" "What do you think the people should have done next?"

   4. *Delving:* "What else happened?" "What else could have happened?" "What do you wish had happened?"

III. *Processing Questions.* Processing questions help students to evaluate and make judgments. Evaluation questions contribute to decision making and problem solving. These questions equip students with valuable thinking skills that help them function in life.

   1. *Personal:* "How can I help you?" "What do you need?" "How do you feel?"

   2. *Monitoring:* "What is happening here?" "Why do you think that way?" "What else could we have done?"

IV. *Learning Questions.* Learning questions promote divergent thinking. Divergent questions introduce creativity, inviting students to use their imaginations and participate based on their individuality. These questions get students to think about what might be or could be possible in ways that may not have been shared during their previous class conversations.

1. *Predicting:* "What is going to happen next?" "If the situation changed, what might have happened?" "What else could the people have tried to solve the problem?"

2. *Concluding:* "What have you learned?" "What would you like to learn?" "Who could you visit to get more information?"

Base Questioning on Taxonomies

Additionally, there are two taxonomies or tables of questions that it is highly recommended you reference frequently when you are crafting your questions in advance of your preassessments, formative, and summative assessments. One taxonomy was published by Bloom et al. in 1956 (see Appendix B for an extensive list of verbs to use when writing learning objectives). This taxonomy identifies six kinds of questions that will diversify and enrich the learning and your teaching in ways that are both effective and efficient. Bloom's six kinds of questions involve

1. *Knowledge:* Identification and recall of information

2. *Comprehension:* Organization and selection of facts and ideas

3. *Application:* Use of facts, rules, and principles

4. *Analysis:* Separation of a whole into parts, components, or categories

5. *Synthesis:* Combinations of ideas to form a whole new idea

6. *Evaluation:* Construction of opinions, judgments, or decisions

Another taxonomy of objectives was developed by Marzano (2000). Marzano's taxonomy is made up of three systems and the knowledge domain, all of which are important for thinking and learning (see Appendix B). The three systems are the self-system, the metacognitive system, and the cognitive system. The self-system focuses the learner on deciding if and when to begin a new task or continue the current one. The metacognitive system helps the learner set goals and keep track of achievement. The cognitive system assists the learner in processing necessary information. Finally, the knowledge domain provides the content.

Marzano's taxonomy offers you a different organization than Bloom's for designing your curriculum, planning your instruction, and conducting your formative assessments. You can check the learning with each system as well as with the knowledge domain. Each of these taxonomies and the verbs in Appendix B will help you to advance and vary your question-asking expertise.

Try Socratic Questioning

Socratic questions help to keep the discussion focused, logical, stimulated, insightful, and inclusive of all learners. The teacher facilitates a shared conversation by asking questions only and not giving answers. This is quite difficult for most teachers. The teacher must be prepared to ask follow-up questions to expand upon the students' responses or absence of responses and motivate students to participate.

Socratic questioning should include

1. Shared goals and objectives to maintain the focus

2. Shared questions and problems to guide the conversation

3. Stimulating and organizing thinking through probing questions

4. Shared concepts and practices to frame the logic

5. Shared information and data to reference throughout the conversation

6. Conversations focused on self-learning

7. Open participation and accepted exchange of expressions ensured by the teacher

8. Open viewpoints for interpreting perspectives

9. Intellectually fair questions and comments

10. Periodic summaries with implications

Here is an example of Socratic questioning in a third grade social studies class studying communities.

Who can give me an example of a service in our community that many people use?

What is one example why people use this service?

Why is it considered a community service?

How do you know that people use this service?

How does this service help the community?

How does this service not help the community?

Why would I ask how this service does not help the community?

What might happen if this service were no longer available?

What is another example why people use this service?

How is this service like the one we just discussed?

How is this service not like the one we just discussed?

Which service do you use most often and why?

Follow Strategic Guidelines in Questioning

You want your questions to be significant, purposeful, relevant, open ended, natural, challenging, and rewarding. Here are some guidelines to help fortify your success throughout the planning, implementation, and assessment.

1. Plan some of your questions in advance of the learning experience. You might want to use the taxonomies in Appendix B as a frame to guarantee that you have included all kinds of questions.

2. As you pose your inquiries, balance fact-seeking questions with thought-provoking questions.

3. Be sure that you ask all kinds of questions of all kinds of learners, and that all learners are ready at all times. Write your students' names on individual cards or sticks; then draw one card or stick when you ask a question. This technique will increase your fairness and objectivity while simultaneously increasing the students' levels of motivation and engagement.

4. However, you want to match the level of question with the level of the learner. You should be ready to modify your questions to fit the learners' ability.

5. Personalize the questions when appropriate. Many times you will know that one particular student has a unique connection to the question.

6. Ask questions using appropriate vocabulary.

7. Keep the questions simple and a reasonable length.

8. If you want learners to respond in a particular format, you should model, reinforce, and use the format.

9. Promote lengthy answers to your questions; avoid one-word and yes/no answers or questions posed as "Who can tell me . . . ?"

10. Follow answers to basic questions by delving. You can ask your learners, "Tell me more . . . ," "How does that work . . . ," "Give me an example . . . ," and so forth.

11. Place the learner in the context of the question. For example, you could ask, "How would you feel if you were that person?" or "What is one way that you could have solved that problem?"

12. Allow time for the learners to hear the question and construct a response. Alternate between calling a learner's name prior to asking the question with not calling a name. There are strengths and weaknesses with each technique.

13. Listen carefully to each student's response. Listen to what the learner is saying and what the learner is not saying. You might be tempted to move along quickly or manage inattentive learners. However, it is essential that you model effective listening and reward the learner appropriately. Ideally, you can ask another student to follow one response with additional responses or explanations. You can ask another student, "What did you think of that response?" "Give us a different possibility . . . ," "What was another idea you gained from the reading?"

14. Help a struggling learner. Avoid letting students get away with responding that they don't know. This is a good time to ask another learner to give a hint or a typical example.

15. Be sure to avoid vague, abstract, or confrontational questions and questions that encourage learners to merely guess, commonly called "Guess What the Teacher Is Thinking."

16. Try not to interrupt or allow other students to interrupt a student who is talking. Let your learners complete their responses. You may have to use a signal to your learners to hang onto their thoughts so everyone receives a chance.

17. Delve fairly with your learners. You want to demonstrate equity based on gender, race/ethnicity, socioeconomics, ability, and so forth.

18. Reroute aggressive, irritating, and negative responses. You can inform a student who responds in this way that you'll check in with her or him later (and be sure you do) or move onto another learner. Avoid responding with sarcasm. (Students will learn more about sarcasm than about the academic subject area.)

19. Announce that the students must ask the questions. Using name cards or name sticks, select a student to ask another student a question. You can post the taxonomies and instruct the learner to ask a particular kind or domain of question. You can use this technique in writing too.

20. This last guideline is the best one. Avoid repeating your questions and the students' answers. These are extremely difficult challenges for teachers, but you are using twice as much time as necessary when you repeat yourself and your learners. Plus, by establishing a learning environment in which students are expected to listen to one another and not wait for you to echo everything that is said in class, you are modeling appreciation of and respect for each student's contribution. When you echo everything that is spoken in class, you establish an environment in which learners are not heard or appreciated by their peers. Ask your questions loudly and clearly; then wait. Call on a student using a fair technique; wait. Delve if needed; wait. Allow for the complete answer; smile and nod. You also do not need to add more explanation to every response. Let your learners inform and support one another.

Optimize the Feedback

As you conduct your formative assessments and engage your students in discussions using all kinds of questioning techniques, you will provide your learners with feedback to promote understanding related to the concepts, skills, and dispositions. Feedback involves your sharing observations, guidance, and support related to a specific event, a series of events, or the overall situation. Feedback may be solicited or volunteered; it may be welcomed or annoying; it may be requested or required. It can be formal and informal; planned and spontaneous; direct and indirect. Feedback can be thoughtful or mindless; helpful or a hindrance; kind or unkind. Throughout your schooling, you have received all aspects of feedback, and now it is essential to consider the roles that feedback plays with your learners.

In the classroom there is a continuous feedback loop between the teacher and learners, between and among the learners themselves, between the teacher and the families, between and among the teacher and colleagues, and between the teacher and the administration. Learning and teaching depend on clear communication, and feedback is always present.

The goals of your feedback to students are to:

1. Build student confidence

2. Identify strengths and weaknesses

3. Include correction and redirection

4. Advance achievement in all domains

5. Assist with clarification

6. Diversify learning experiences

7. Communicate positive and motivating support

8. Offer productive and practical ideas

9. Improve performance

10. Promote accountability

As one teacher shared:

Negative feedback is worse than no feedback.

Effective feedback should be

1. *Timely.* Feedback should be given and received as close as possible to the observation and interaction; each of us wants to know how well we are progressing and if correction would be helpful.

2. *Specific.* Feedback should be objective and describe a particular event or series of events based on measurable assessments. Feedback should not be subjective or vague or based merely on feelings and intuition. Start with positive recognition of progress or production and follow with correction or redirection. Avoid negative confrontation.

3. *Purposeful.* Feedback should be helpful and contribute to growth, development, and change that benefits everyone involved. Feedback also needs to be friendly, kind, and supportive.

4. *Two way.* Feedback from teachers to learners may be shared with individuals, small groups, or the whole class. Once teachers have shared, then the learner(s) must be provided opportunities to share. Teachers are encouraged to let students share first so teachers can assess the situation in advance of correction and redirection.

5. *Understood.* Feedback must be checked. Teachers can ask learners to show them the modifications or revise the outcomes. Teachers also should model understanding by restating what the teacher has heard and confirming what the student will do to demonstrate changes. Modeling is essential for learners to observe understanding for themselves.

6. *Reassessed.* Feedback must be assessed or checked again for long-term acquisition, appreciation, and appreciation. This is exactly the reason for formative assessments. They inform the learner and teacher as each person is forming.

Refine Correction and Redirection

From the feedback you receive from your learners, you will discover who is "getting it" and who is not. Now is the time to correct students if they have learned a concept or skill inaccurately or improperly and to redirect them if they are headed on a path that will not benefit or maximize their learning. For example, if the objective of your learning experience is placing words in alphabetical order, you conduct your baseline preassessment to organize expectations as you design curriculum and instruction and align assessments. Then you collect your formative assessments, and you receive and give feedback. You begin to level the learning and teaching.

This is when correction and redirection occur. You have demonstrated how to alphabetize according to the first few letters of the word. Then you discover that some of your learners are not applying the skill beyond the first letter. These learners need correction so that they alphabetize accurately. You also discover that some of your learners are confused about alphabetizing words that start with *Mc* versus *Mac,* so you redirect the learning.

There are many ways to implement correction and redirection. You want to select the most appropriate way and yet use a variety of ways during the school year. The way you guide correction and redirection with your learners will influence them throughout their lives, both in and out of school. You want correction and redirection to be positive and productive. After all, we all make mistakes, and some of the best learning comes from our mistakes.

Your corrections and redirections can address:

1. *Accuracy.* The teacher gives the correct information; for example, "A comma goes here." "The sum is 14." "The planet Neptune should have been included in this diagram."

2. *Modeling.* The teacher restates the information accurately without identifying what is incorrect, with appropriate emphasis on the correction; for example, when the student says, "The boy done his homework," The teacher responds, "Tell me how the boy did his homework."

3. *Precision.* The teacher encourages the learner to be meticulous; for example, "Look at the sentence and read it again carefully." "What is another way of finding the information faster and more easily?"

4. *Clarification.* The teacher asks for more information without identifying what is incorrect; for example, "I didn't quite hear you; please pronounce the word again." "Find the place in the story that tells us what the man was doing."

5. *Relevance.* The teacher narrows the conversation with the learner to the most important or meaningful pieces of information or parts of the process; for example, "Let's look at what the author tells us." "How does your answer fit with the question?"

6. *Logic.* The teacher guides the learning to include reason and common sense; for example, "What would most people do in that situation?" "Tell me the first thing that usually happens when that event occurs."

7. *Breadth.* The teacher broadens the learning to include more ideas; for example, "Tell me about the other children in the story." "What are some similar items we could place in that category?"

8. *Depth.* The teacher digs into the complexities of a topic or issue; for example, "Think a little more here and write more steps in your directions." "What other reasons are responsible for this reaction?"

9. *Challenge.* The teacher questions the thinking without identifying what is incorrect; for example, "Do you think that is the reason the girl swam across the river?" "Does that solution make sense?"

10. *Elicitation.* The teacher encourages and prompts the learner to try again without identifying what is incorrect; for example, "Look at the title of the page and read the sentence again." "Be sure you have included all of the pieces of the puzzle."

11. *Repetition.* The teacher repeats the incorrect item as a question without identifying what is incorrect; for example, "Fish are mammals?" "4 × 5 = 25?"

12. *Resources.* The teacher asks the learner who gave the incorrect item where the learner could find the correct response; for example, "That is not quite right; where in the classroom can you find the correct answer?" "You are close; what could you check to fix your error?"

13. *Extension.* The teacher refers to a different example to help the learner see a pattern; for example, "Let's look at the grid together and see where to place the coordinates correctly." "What is another word that is a possessive plural so we can fix the first word?"

14. *Peers.* The teacher instructs another student to help the student who has given the incorrect response; for example, "Averie, please give Kim a hint to that question." "Josh, what did you include in your chart that might help Jamie?"

15. *Revision.* The teacher identifies what is incorrect and asks the learner to revise and redo the task; for example, "Caroline, you have only one misspelled word in your paragraph; please find the correct spelling and show me your paper." "Dustin, that is not London; please look carefully at the map and find London."

16. *Significance.* The teacher probes the outcomes with the learner to identify the most important portion of the process and/or product; for example, "What was a high point of this experience for you?" "What will you remember from this unit of learning?"

Table 5.4 presents a list of all 16 types of intervention strategies.

Table 5.4   Intervention Strategies to Correct and Redirect Learning

1. Accuracy	9. Challenge
2. Modeling	10. Elicitation
3. Precision	11. Repetition
4. Clarification	12. Resources
5. Relevance	13. Extension
6. Logic	14. Peers
7. Breadth	15. Revision
8. Depth	16. Significance

Use Interventions

Research shows that planning for prevention can eliminate or reduce the need for intervention (Brown-Chidsey, 2007); the three approaches include:

1. *Primary prevention* stops an unwanted or inappropriate action from occurring. For example: With the assistance of the students, the teacher lists the steps for completing the assignment on the board prior to the start of the activity.

2. *Secondary prevention* addresses a particular concern or symptom when it first appears. For example: As students attempt to complete an assignment, the teacher reviews the first item with the whole class and writes the correct answer on the board.

3. *Tertiary prevention* is applied when the concern has manifested itself wholly. For example: After reading the students' answers to an assignment, the teacher discusses possible solutions with the whole class as a learning experience beneficial for the next attempt.

Once preventative measures are in place, there are four tiers of intervention to practice when responding to learners as you collect assessments and provide feedback:

1. Regular *standards-based* classroom interactions through which learners meet expectations at minimum proficiency

2. Focused *needs-based* assistance for learners who have not met expectations at minimum proficiency

3. *Support team* assistance for learners who need additional and more intense assistance when they significantly do not meet expectations at minimum proficiency; interventions may be conducted in the regular classroom or in a resource classroom

4. Specially designed *learning environments* for learners who need adapted programs and classrooms

Involve Your Learners in the Process

Within every learning experience and unit of learning, you want to plan for motivating your learners and empowering them through active engagement and decision making. To achieve these goals, you must explore your students' interests, so that the learning and teaching are truly about them.

Once you become aware and comfortable with formative assessments, you can involve your learners in the process too. You will conduct formative assessments examining your learners' interests primarily through spoken communications. As you open a conversation with links to your learners' immediate world, your learners will race to their classroom every day at the right time to become an active part of your learning community. If you motivate them, they will come.

The learning takes on a whole new dimension when you connect the new learning with your students' immediate world. For example, through your formative assessments, you can discover how the content fits with their thoughts, feelings, and activities both at school and out of school. Pose some fascinating questions, wait, and listen. Place your learners in small groups; give them some colorful paper to record some notes. Ask them to write lists of items or to draw some pictures. Your learners will talk with one another and share all kinds of personal interests. You will gain assorted insights to your learners when you give them the chance to talk.

Students can complete self-assessments and peer assessments. They can even help you write the assessment items. For example, your ninth graders are going to write a movie review. You and your learners develop the expectations that should be included in each paragraph. You record the expectations on a sheet of paper, copy the paper, and distribute it to the learners when they have written the first drafts of their movie reviews.

Then learners can assess their own progress or assess a peer's paragraph before producing the final copy. Together you and your learners create the list of expectations and conduct the formative assessment. You can apply this process to any part of your curriculum and instruction. Just think how much your students will learn about themselves and improve their levels of performance when they are in charge.

Figure 5.1 illustrates the circular sequence of designing curriculum, aligning assessments, and assigning instruction.

Have Fun With Formative Assessments . . .

The first time I suggested to my university students that they could, and should, have fun with their assessments, I thought I had released a cage of snakes. The students actually hissed at me. Most teachers have not been prepared to understand and use assessments, yet every teacher assesses. Teachers may think of their assessments only as summative or end points, yet your students can double their learning if you incorporate learning, feedback, and correction that builds upon the formative assessments in ways that are positive, purposeful, and productive.

Instead of getting frustrated that your learners are not "getting it," observe, listen, converse, interact, read, and reflect with your learners. They will tell you what they know and can do; they will tell you what they want to know and do. They want to learn and do well; they want to please their families and be recognized by their friends. Conducting appropriate formative assessments to monitor progress is the solution.

Think of it like eating in a restaurant: you want to be satisfied completely. You want the ideal restaurant near you and one that serves the kind of foods you are seeking, hygienically, attractively, and quickly. You want a comfortable seat with a great view. You want delicious food prepared to your preferences. You want to enjoy your company and the environment. You want your cognitive, psychomotor, affective, and psychosocial domains fulfilled.

Before the meal begins, the host may welcome you, ask you where you want to sit, and make an initial inquiry as to what you are in the mood to eat or drink. You provide answers as a form of feedback. You

Figure 5.1   Sequence of Designing Curriculum, Aligning Assessments, and Assigning Instruction

1. Design curriculum
2. Align assessments
3. Observe actions, reactions, and interactions
4. Ask questions
5. Listen to responses
6. Gather data
7. Record progress
8. Plan instruction
9. Emphasize thinking
10. Assign activities
11. Share outcomes
12. Present products and projects
13. Record progress
14. Read responses
15. Record progress
16. Provide feedback
17. Modify expectations
18. Refine corrections
19. Monitor redirections
20. Conduct conferences
21. Maintain records
22. Report outcomes
23. Reflect on progress
24. Redesign curriculum
25. Modify assessments
26. Begin new learning experiences and units of learning

give much more feedback as you place your order. These processes are preassessment. During the meal, the server asks you about the meal. This is formative assessment. Now is the time for you to give feedback to request changes for which the server or chef makes corrections. Usually, the server will reassess the redirection. As you are leaving, someone at the front door may inquire about your dining experience. This is summative assessment. Now is the chance for you to give more feedback.

We hope that everyone has fun at the restaurant. You enjoy a fabulous meal and your server receives a fabulous tip.

Extend With Questions and Activities

Frequently Asked Questions

1. How difficult is it to redesign my curriculum and reorganize my instruction to use the learning approaches to formative assessments?

Start slowly and gradually. Select one of the approaches and try it for several weeks. Then either select or add another approach to learning. You should notice immediate changes in your learners. Students like it when the routine is modified and is more student centered.

2. How can I keep track of the changes in my formative assessments?

Keep a spreadsheet on your computer. List the unit of learning, the goals and objects to meet the state standards, and learning expectations. Then list the curriculum, instruction, and assessments— before, during, and after the learning. You will be pleasantly surprised to reflect upon your records and notice which learning approaches and formative assessments fit you, your learners, and each unit of learning.

3. What are the most important results of using formative assessments and using them appropriately?

You will increase your learners' achievement, connections, and satisfaction almost immediately. Your learners will notice that you are right with them. Simultaneously, your teaching will increase in achievement, connections, and satisfaction. What more could teachers or learners want?

Activities

1. Select three of your favorite units of learning and match different approaches to learning with each unit.

2. Look at the schedule for one day in your classroom. Connect a different thinking skill to each activity throughout the day.

3. Brainstorm activities that you usually include in your classroom to showcase each thinking skill.

4. Place each of the 10 ways to correct and redirect learning on a note card. Keep the note cards handy as you interact with your learners. Draw a different note card for each time you want to correct and redirect to see if that would be a way you would select and how it feels to use it in that situation.

5. Tell your learners that you want them to help one another more often. Explain to them that you want them (1) to think about their question, (2) check the resources, (3) ask a friend, and (4) come to the teacher. See if this increases independence, achievement, and satisfaction.

6

Administering Summative Assessments

When I began teaching, I would use the tests that came with the book. My students did not do very well, and, sadly, I found myself teaching to the test so they would raise scores rather than increase understanding. . . . I realized that I should plan my unit by looking at the concepts, vocabulary, activities, and assignments all at once. Then I could write my own unit tests to match the plan before I taught the unit. My students did much, much better . . . and they learned. I was a much happier teacher too.

Summative assessments provide you with data to end a learning experience or unit of learning. It is essential to keep in mind that the end is only temporary. Most likely, you will revisit the learning throughout the year, perhaps as soon as the next day or during the next learning experience. For example, after you end your science unit on the five senses, you will reference the unit outcomes throughout the school year as prior knowledge and experiences. Building upon your own teaching is how you scaffold, spiral, compact, and integrate learning across the curriculum, as described in Chapter 5.

Connect to the Goals and Components of Assessment

As you administer your summative assessments, you collect and analyze data to accomplish three goals:

1. Exchange feedback and provide correction to the learning for the whole class as well as for individual students; although this is the end of the learning experience or unit for now, you may need to intervene and remediate if knowledge, skills, and dispositions are unsatisfactory; this is summative assessment *as* learning.

2. Plan how to modify and adjust future teaching of this learning experience or unit of learning as well as your teaching expertise in general; this is summative assessment *for* learning.

3. Amass continuous data to inform and support knowledge, skills, and dispositions so you can note the progress you and your learners achieve after the learning and teaching; this is summative assessment *of* learning.

Figure 6.1 presents an illustration of your summative assessment. Notice that the labels inside each of the circles read "ends . . . for now,"

Figure 6.1   Summative Assessment Goals

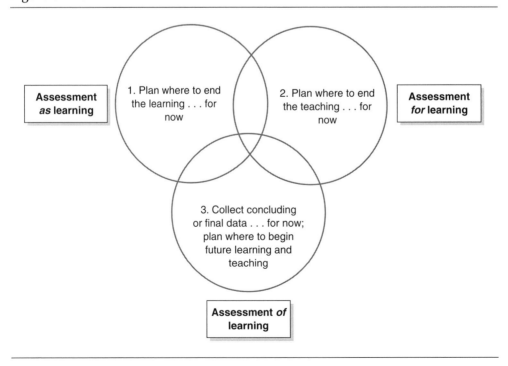

just as they did for formative assessments. To complete the full cycle, summative data becomes baseline and formative data leading to upcoming learning experience and units of learning.

Again, let's revisit the six components of assessment (refer to Figure 1.1 in Chapter 1). Ask yourself the questions in Table 6.1 to guide you as you start to plan and develop your summative assessments to check the learning outcomes and provide concluding feedback to your learners and guidance for yourself.

Create Your Summative Assessments

Summative assessments include tests, in addition to a wide variety of written products, projects, presentations, and portfolios. Generally speaking, in middle-level and secondary school classrooms there are only three ways to assess: watching, listening, and reading, so everything your learners produce will be something you see, something you hear, and/or something you read.

Diversify Outcomes

Summative assessments that you *observe* include learner performances such as writing a word or sentence; solving a problem showing each of the steps; pointing to a letter, word, or number on a chart; finding a location on a map or in a book; demonstrating the parts of an experiment; modeling good citizenship; and so forth. All of these assessments require you to watch closely and record completeness and accuracy (without becoming distracted).

Summative assessments that you *hear* include learner performances such as reading a word, sentence, or passage aloud; telling the steps of the problems; saying the letter, word, or number on the chart; announcing the location on a map or in a book; articulating the parts of an experiment; describing good citizenship; and so forth. All of these assessments require you to listen carefully and record completeness and accuracy (without interrupting).

Summative assessments that you *read* include learner performances that are written and that you read immediately or at a later time, depending on the situation. Each of these assessments also could involve a written portion. A learner can write letters, words, sentences, stories, reports, journals, and so forth, in any kind of context for all subject areas. You decide the most appropriate summative assessment to align with your curriculum and instruction.

Table 6.2 presents examples of summative assessment data for each of the six assessment components.

Table 6.1 Summative Assessment Questions for the Six Components of Assessment

Component of Assessment	Summative Assessment Questions
1. Each learner's individuality and background	a. How have each student's knowledge, skills, and attitudes about cultural characteristics changed? b. How have the learning styles of each student been modified and enhanced? c. How have the personal interests of each student been enriched and expanded?
2. Learner's prior knowledge and experiences	a. What has each student achieved related to the objective? b. What does each student want to learn next related to the objective? What does the class want to learn next? c. How has each student expanded his or her skills for engaging with the outcomes and other learners?
3. Teacher's expertise and expectations	a. What has become your developed expertise related to the content and processes? Do you have a favorite area or a special interest or skill? What have become the unique experiences that enhance and enrich the learning? b. What knowledge, skills, and dispositions guide the learning experience or unit? c. What knowledge, skills, and dispositions guide the integration across the curriculum and make connections outside of the classroom?
4. Teacher's organization and readiness	a. What has become the objective? b. What have become the most effective and efficient ways to facilitate the learning? c. What additional resources are necessary to expand your expertise and readiness?
5. Curricular content and academic standards	a. How will you connect the learning expectations with the student' prior learning in the future? b. How will you ensure that the learning is student centered, student directed, engaging, and providing them with multiple ways to express their learning and exchange ideas in the future? c. How will you make the learning meaningful and relevant in the future?
6. Learning community context	a. How will you establish a community of learners in your classroom to connect with the objective in the future? b. How will you connect learning expectations with the class in the future? c. How will you connect student learning with the world around them in the future?

Table 6.2 Examples of Summative Assessments for the Six Components of Assessment

Componenet of Assessment	Summative Assessment Data
1. Each learner's individuality and background	• Posttest that matches the pretest/preassessment data and formative data • Individual conference • Learner-selected piece of evidence
2. Learner's prior knowledge and experiences	• Final papers, projects, portfolios, and/or presentations as a capstone to the goals and objectives • Conversation in class • KWHL chart (concentrating on what was *learned*)
3. Teacher's expertise and expectations	• Reprioritization of content • Reprioritization of methods • Reprioritization of resources
4. Teacher's organization and readiness	• Posttest that matches the pretest/preassessment data and formative data • Conversation in class • KWHL chart (concentrating on what was *learned*)
5. Curricular content and academic standards	• Evaluation and redesign curricular mapping for one learning experience • Evaluation and redesign curricular mapping for a unit of learning • Evaluation and redesign curricular mapping that scaffold, spiral, and compact learning
6. Learning community context	• Evaluation and redesign of technique for building community • Evaluation and redesign of technique for connecting learning to prior learning • Evaluation and redesign of technique for connecting learning to the real world

Organize Projects and Presentations

Projects and presentations make the learning come alive in your classroom. The challenge is establishing expectations and scoring outcomes. There are two approaches that you can use separately or combined: analytic and holistic.

Begin by writing a description of the final outcomes and identifying the academic standards that provide the constructs of the curriculum design guiding the project or presentation. You must be able to rationalize why you are undertaking this endeavor. Then write the details of your instruction and the activities you will assign contributing to the outcomes. Now you are ready to align your assessment.

Most likely, the project or presentation will include several parts. When you score each part of the project, your assessment is *analytic.* When you score only the overall outcome, your assessment is *holistic.* Remember, you may choose one approach, the other, or both. Most middle-level and secondary school teachers use both assessments. The teachers want to give feedback on each part of the project as well as on the final production.

If your approach is analytic, you want to write an individual assessment for each part so you can provide the type of feedback that is appropriate for that part. Give the anticipated assessment to your learners when announcing the assignment. For example, your assignment is to prepare a five-part report on a famous U.S. citizen. Part I introduces the individual through a biography. Part II highlights the individual's contributions. Part III summarizes the individual's legacy over time. Part IV includes a timeline of the individual's life, and Part V is a picture of the individual with pictures of that individual's major contributions.

You develop analytic assessments for each part of the project so the learners and their families understand exactly what is expected, when it is expected, why this assignment is being made, and how the learner will be assessed. With projects and presentations that learners prepare even partially at home, you also want to set the parameters and limitations. Some families will offer seemingly unending assistance and ideas. Consider how much families can assist their children and how families can share clever ideas with you.

Feature Portfolios

Many teachers and schools feature portfolios to assemble their learners' papers for sharing with families at curriculum fairs and parent-teacher conferences. Portfolios have been used forever by artists and architects. Portfolios can be created for individual students, to showcase student work, as resources for teachers, and to note specific institutional development.

Teachers and learners can determine collaboratively the required and optional items or artifacts to be kept in the portfolio. As the fair or conference nears, the teacher and learners can practice how the materials in the portfolios will be shared with the specified audience. The portfolio is the ideal mechanism through which learners can see changes over time and gain a sense of self-assessment. Students can easily showcase their accomplishments with other people by showing and telling about each artifact and reflecting on the process.

Teachers need to make sure that learners have voice, choice, and agency in their portfolios. This means that each learner actively participates in the planning, organization, and selection of artifacts so the student develops a sense of ownership and, it is hoped, pride. You can address everyday items and special selections to include written, auditory, and visual products. Portfolios can be subdivided to fit your needs. Assembling a portfolio is a continuous process, and the learners must be closely involved and consulted from the start.

You can decide whether you want to assess individual artifacts as they are completed or assess all of them at once to evaluate the entire portfolio. Your decision will depend on your learners' experiences with portfolios, your purposes for maintaining portfolios, and when and with whom the portfolio artifacts will be shared.

Portfolios are perfect for conducting self-assessments by the learners and assessments by the parents. Together with your learners, you can develop checklists and/or rubrics to guide you through the assessment processes.

You will be required to create ways of storing the growing portfolios. As they become expanding accordions, perhaps you will want to design a common frame of organization and a table of contents so learners can quickly access the artifacts that they want to share at the fair or conferences.

Write Meaningful and Purposeful Assessments

Your assignments must include clear directions. Try writing your directions, then asking a colleague or perhaps a friend who is not a teacher to follow your directions. Using a peer review process will make a huge difference in communicating your expectations to your learners and their families. Remember, many of your assignments and assessments will be reviewed by your learners' families, so you are always writing for them too.

As you write your assessments, particularly test items, you want to be sure that you are seeking understanding related to the knowledge, skills, and dispositions that you expect your students to have practiced and mastered. Use developmentally appropriate vocabulary; keep the items short and direct; avoid confusing questions, especially questions with double negatives.

Although you want your learners to be successful, watch out for giving confusing hints and clues. This tends to happen frequently with both written and oral questioning. The assessment evolves into a game in which the learner is trying to find the patterns rather than answering the questions. Be aware of your patterns for answers to the multiple choice questions too.

As you lay out the assessment on paper, you want to leave plenty of space for learners to record answers and construct essays. Avoid splitting items from front to back or page to page. Also avoid place the word bank on one page and placing the items referencing the word bank on another page. Number the test items and the pages.

Try completing your own summative assessments, especially the tests, as if you were one of your students. Take a moment to review the salience, reliability, validity, fidelity, and robustness as described in Chapter 1. Reflect on these questions: *Are the questions and expectations reasonable? Do the questions and assignments include all of Bloom's and Marzano's taxonomies* (see Chapter 5)*? Are there questions or tasks that ask learners to personalize answers and connect with the real world outside of the classroom?*

Prepare Learners for Summative Assessments

You want your learners to do well on your summative assessments, so teach them how to succeed. Table 6.3 presents a list of guidelines you may want to read aloud to your students. When you are administering summative assessments that feature tests, be sure that the classroom is quiet and everything nonessential has been put away. Help your learners to monitor the time and complete the task. Provide a silent activity for learners who finish the task before the rest of the learners. Decide if you want learners to bring their finished assessments and tests to you, to leave them on their desks, or to raise their hands so you can collect the tests. Most likely, you can move around the classroom with less noise or interruption than most of your learners and you can monitor completion at the same time.

You want to minimize cheating by watching your learners during the entire test-taking time period. If your students are prone to cheating, most likely you will start recognizing the patterns in your classroom early during the school year. Then you can intervene and interrupt the cheating possibilities appropriately.

Table 6.3   Guidelines for Completing Summative Assessments and Taking Tests

1. Write your name, date, and other required information on the test in the proper space before reading the directions.

2. Read all directions carefully and completely before starting the test.

3. Notice how responses should be recorded and how they will be scored, that is, do grammar, spelling, punctuation, and so forth count?

4. Check the time in which you are allowed to complete the test so you can pace yourself.

5. If possible, complete sections of the test with selected responses first so you refresh your vocabulary.

6. Second, complete sections of the test with constructed essays. Plan your essays by constructing an outline on a separate piece of paper before writing on the test. Remember to reference the vocabulary in the selected response section of the test.

7. If you record your answers on a separate sheet, be sure that you are making answers in the correct location.

8. Complete as much of the test as you can. Guessing at an answer is better than leaving an item blank.

9. Proofread the entire test before giving it to the teacher. You might want to pretend that you are taking the test all over again. Be sure to look at the back side of each sheet of paper.

10. Try to get plenty of rest, eat well, and relax so you are ready for the test. Avoid last-minute late-night cramming for the test.

Score Assessments Objectively

Once you have received the assessments, your challenge is to score them fairly and objectively. You want to be sure that you maintain *rater reliability*. That means that (1) all assessments are scored with the same expectations, (2) the assessment would receive the same score regardless of who scores it, and (3) if the same assessment is administered to the same or similar group of learners at another time by the same raters, the assessments would be scored with the same expectations.

Here are some guidelines to assist with this process. Begin by completing the assessment yourself and making an answer key for the selected responses. Then construct three sets of answers for the short answers and essays. You want to establish sample benchmarks that you consider proficient (high), satisfactory (medium), and unsatisfactory (low) and the number of points each answer will earn. Before you score the learners' assessments, decide whether grammar, punctuation, capitalization, and spelling are required for each category, along with other expected details.

Try to score the essays without looking at the students' names. You can use a code for the entire paper or ask for names to be written on another side of the page. Score all of the responses to one short answer or essay question at a time so you can compare and contrast all of the answers. If you are getting tired, stop and take a break once you have scored all of the same short answer or essay questions for the entire class.

Once the assessments have been scored, conduct an item analysis. If many or all of your students missed the same questions, look carefully at those particular items to see if the items were worded clearly and tested information the learners should have answered correctly. You may want to remove frequently missed items from the final analysis. This is your opportunity to reteach missed material and to improve your future summative assessments and test writing as well as to enhance your learners' summative assessment preparation and test taking.

Understand Standardized Testing

Although they are not considered a performance-based assessment, let's briefly address standardized testing, as this represents another and important summative assessment that will play a significant role in your career. Most nationalized standardized tests are commercially produced and include both criterion-referenced and norm-referenced assessments. Since you cannot view standardized tests prior to their distribution and are unable to make and keep copies to guide classroom learning, the criteria for the tests—unlike most criterion-referenced assessments you will use in your classroom—is unknown in advance of the testing. Over time, students tend to improve their test scores; naturally, when teachers administer the standardized tests, they see the test items and may be able to remember them to incorporate into their instruction. To prevent this, standardized tests are re-normed from time to time. A new set of test items is developed so learners cannot be prepared specifically for a particular test.

The results of standardized tests (and other assessments) are reported in six ways:

1. *Raw scores:* The total number of responses answered correctly or incorrectly; there are no bases of relationship to the total possible (that is, the number correct equals 20; the number incorrect equals 5)

2. *Percentages:* The total number of responses answered correctly or incorrectly in relationship to the total possible (that is, the number correct—20 out of 25—equals 80 percent, or the number incorrect—5 out of 25—equals 20 percent)

3. *Percentiles:* The total number of responses answered correctly or incorrectly in relationship to the total possible and to the percentages earned by all individuals taking the same test (that is, the number correct for one individual: 20 out of 25; all of the percentages listed and divided into equal tenths or percentiles)

4. *Quartiles:* The total number of responses answered correctly or incorrectly in relationship to the total possible and to the percentages earned by all individuals taking the same test (that is, the number correct for one individual: 20 out of 25; all of the percentages listed and divided into equal fourths or quartiles)

5. *Rates:* All of the percentages listed from best to worst, identifying the number of tests earning the same percentage (that is, if 4 of the 20 tests earned an 80 percent, then 80 percent would receive a 20 percent of all of the test scores; the rating percentage is relative to the distribution of all scores)

6. *Ranks:* All of the percentages listed from best to worst, identifying the placement or rank in the list (that is, 80 percent ranks number 2; the ranking is relative to the distribution of all scores)

Standardized test items include all kinds of selected responses. Test takers pick the right or best answers to a variety of multiple choice items. Some schools dedicate more time and effort to test-taking skills and test preparation using commercially prepared materials that match the test; other schools do not. You need to follow the leadership at your school. And school administrators will guide you with all the details for sharing outcomes with learners and their families.

Ultimately, your mission is to design your curriculum, assign your instruction and activities, and align your performance-based assessments so that all your learners are as well prepared as possible for the standardized test. As best you can, keep in mind that standardized tests are just a snapshot in the much larger picture of assessment.

Set Your Sights on the Five As

Here are five essential guidelines for you to follow when constructing effective summative assessments. Each of the five guidelines may seem obvious, yet far too many teachers overlook their importance to learners' and to their own success. Ask yourself some powerful questions as you check to see if your assessments fulfill and how they satisfy the five *A*s of assessment:

1. Academic rigor

2. Active learning

3. Authenticity

4. Alternatives

5. Achievement

Strive for Academic Rigor

Academic rigor is a phrase frequently used by educators and families. However, everyone seems to different definitions, manifestations, and priorities associated with the phrase. In general, academic rigor is multifaceted and encompasses the curriculum, instructional, assessments, context, management, and community. Academic rigor involves establishing, maintaining, and communicating high standards and expectations for all students that are constructed, generated, and reviewed by everyone.

The Bill and Melinda Gates Foundation has adopted six clusters of competence (Priesz, 2006) that define academic rigor, including:

1. *Literacy.* All learners demonstrate that they are capable of a working command of reading, writing, and speaking English.

2. *Mathematical competence.* All learners demonstrate that they are able to exhibit a command of the basic computational skills required in the workplace and in everyday adult life.

3. *Problem solving.* All learners demonstrate that they are eager to seek out information, discover answers, and apply their skills in reasoning and critical thinking to solve problems.

4. *Scientific literacy.* All learners demonstrate that they are capable of appreciating nature and the environment, are familiar with the scientific method and the role of science in modern life, and are cognizant of the uncertainties of the scientific method.

5. *Good citizenship.* All learners demonstrate that they are well grounded in the forces and values that have shaped this nation historically, culturally, demographically, politically, and economically, with an appreciation for the relationships of the United States to the rest of the world and the U. S.'s role in the world.

6. *Technological advancement.* All learners demonstrate that they are comfortable with technology and capable of using it in the normal course of everyday work and learning.

Academic rigor must serve all learners; involve the four domains of learning (cognitive, psychomotor, affective, and psychosocial; see Chapter 2); offer relevant opportunities to express and exchange outcomes with and among other learners; connect within and across the curriculum as well into the community and world; prepare learners for lifelong learning and living; support learners, their families, teachers, and administrators through meaningful relations so everyone feels recognized and respected.

Your summative assessments not only align with your objectives and performance expectations, they match your scoring or grading systems. This means that when you introduce a learning experience or unit of learning, you describe it as an entire package. You tell your students what they are going to learn, how they are going to show you their accomplishments both along the way (formative assessments) and at the end (summative assessments). Prior to the learning and teaching, you identify the benchmarks or various levels of outcomes for your learners and perhaps their families. Many times, you will need to construct some sample benchmarks so you are assured that your expectations include rigor, relevance, and relationships for every learner.

Table 6.4 presents a specific example of a rubric with rigor for a unit on parables that includes cognitive, psychomotor, affective, and psychosocial domains. The teacher identifies and communicates expectations for the acquisition, application, appreciation, and adaptation (Daggett, 2005) of the academic rigor by the learners. Keep in mind that you want your students to relate learning to

- More than one academic discipline,
- Higher-order thinking skills that include problem solving and decision making, and
- Habits of mind and work required to complete complex and creative tasks.

Table 6.4 Academic Rigor: Rubric for a Unit About Parables

Exceeds Expectations	*Meets Expectations*	*Does Not Meet Expectations*
Reads more than 5 parables silently and aloud in class	Reads 3–4 parables silently and aloud in class	Reads fewer than 3 parables silently and aloud in class
With a partner, writes own parable with a logical and exciting beginning, middle, and end	With a partner, writes own parable with a logical beginning, middle, and end	With a partner, writes own parable with a start at a beginning, middle, and end
Follows all the writing guidelines	Follows most the writing guidelines	Follows some, but not all, of the writing guidelines
Reads parable aloud to class with feeling	Reads parable aloud to class	Does not read parable aloud
Reads 3–4 parables aloud at home and returns signed note	Reads 3–4 parables aloud at home and returns signed note	Reads fewer than 3 parables aloud at home and returns signed note

Promote Active Learning and Assessments

Consider these revealing percentages. In general, learners remember approximately:

10 percent of what they hear

20 percent of what they read

30 percent of what they see

40 percent of what they hear and see

50 percent of what they discuss

60 percent of what they hear, read, see, and discuss

70 percent of what they do

80 percent of what they use

90 percent of what they teach

It seems rather obvious that you want your students to get involved in their learning all the way through, from preassessment to summative assessment. Engage your learners through every domain to immerse themselves in the learning. When you introduce a new topic or issue, ask your students what they want to learn and record it on a large sheet of paper that you post in the classroom. Incorporate what they want to learn with what you need them to learn. Then ask your learners how they want to proceed.

Let your students organize their own explorations and share their own discoveries with all the other students. This will change them and you forever. First, you will empower your learners to take charge of their own learning. Second, you will increase the learning in your classrooms more than you can ever imagine. Third, you don't have to do all the work preparing for others; you construct together. Fourth, you create a community of learners preparing for their own futures— a world that is not yet defined. Fifth, your learners transfer the outcomes from one learning experience to the next, transforming school into an inviting, igniting, and exciting laboratory.

Keep a list of the various ways students engage in their learning so you can nurture and nudge them collectively and individually throughout the school year. Talk with your colleagues, especially colleagues in the fine arts, to find other approaches for integrating the curriculum. You will be pleasantly surprised when the fine art teachers want to collaborate; after all, they share the same challenges that you face.

Table 6.5 presents a variety of summative assessment ideas that involve active learning.

Ensure Authentic Outcomes

Summative assessments based on high standards and active engagement in the investigations and discoveries must be authentic. You want your formative and your summative assessments to check students' learning in ways that are logical and meaningful. For example, when you are teaching your students computer skills, the students need to be able to use computers, and frequently. Learners want and need time to become familiar with the machinery, the functions, and the possibilities. They need opportunities to explore computers on their own and with peers. This is the perfect example of a time to let your learners teach one another (and maybe you). Playing a computer game and surfing the Internet are authentic assessments. When your learners can demonstrate their proficiencies in ways they are comfortable and confident, then you have accomplished the competence you want to see.

When conducting science experiments, let learners guide the experiments in the classroom and in real life. For example, when making the chemical compounds found in fire extinguishers, practice

Table 6.5   Summative Assessment Ideas for Active Learning

Ads	Internet messages	Pictures
Agendas	Internet searches	Plans
Artwork	Inventions	Plays
Blueprints	Inventions (plans)	Poetry
Books	Inventory	Problem solutions
Calendars	Jokes	Problems
Cartoons	Journals	Puppet shows
Collections	Journeys	Recipes
Commercials	Letters	Scale models
Dances	Maps	Scientific lab report
Designs	Menus	Scripts
Diaries	Models (constructed)	Skits
Directions	Musical compositions	Steps to follow
Documentaries	Musical presentations	Stories
Drawings	Musical scores	Story boards
Experiments	Notebooks	Story illustrations
Files	Oral readings	Timelines
Folders	Oral reports	Travel brochures
Foreign language words	Pantomimes	Word banks
Games	Photographs	

using a fire extinguisher. After using math manipulatives, transfer the learning to the world around you. Measure the soccer field or school cafeteria. To combine math and science in learning about the environment, measure the waste in the class wastebasket every day and predict the amount of waste generated in a week or a month. Then measure to compare and contrast the actual amounts with the predicted amounts.

Each of these summative assessments and the ones listed in Table 6.5 showcase learners' multiple intelligences (Gardner, 1993). The eight intelligences describe different ways that individuals think, act, and feel. Although each student possesses aspects of all eight intelligences, it is believed that each learner possesses a dominant intelligence or a greater strength in one specific form of intelligence. Teachers are encouraged to be aware of the eight intelligences, to incorporate all eight intelligences in the classroom, to find ways to link each student with his or her strength, and to seek additional information and support relating to a student with a specific intelligence. Performance-based assessments demonstrated as summative assessments give you and your learners authentic feedback related to each of the eight intelligences. The eight multiple intelligences, their meanings, and examples of summative assessments across the curriculum are presented in Appendix B.

Instead of saying *somewhere, someday,* and *somehow* when facilitating your learning experiences, consider ways to make them here-and-now with real applications. Network with your colleagues for strategies; search the Internet for ideas; ask your learners' families to donate materials. Again, you don't have to do all the work.

Include Alternative Approaches

You want to keep track of the kinds of formative and summative assessments you use. Your challenge is to balance an assortment of assessments that helps establish a comfortable routine but does not become a stale rut. For some parts of your curriculum and instruction, you want to establish a regular pattern. For example, many middle-level and secondary school teachers follow a pattern for learning the weekly vocabulary words, such as Monday is the pretest and practice of missed words; Tuesday is the activity to learn the week's vocabulary topic in concept; Wednesday is an application of the vocabulary in content; Thursday is the final test; and Friday is the repeated practice of missed words for future testing. Some schools have adopted a schoolwide program so the families can help their children learn the weekly words.

While this type of repetitive approach may work for vocabulary and some other subject areas, you want to showcase alternative approaches, including all kinds of performance-based assessments, for many of your learning experiences and units of learning. Now is the time to have fun and expand your repertoire. Let your learners:

- Present about something they have learned
- Chart or graph data to explain a situation

- Participate in a debate to defend a viewpoint on an issue
- Act out a scene from a book
- Serve on a committee to make a decision
- Read the news over the intercom
- Teach others (perhaps younger students in another grade level) about a topic to show their knowledge and skills

Notice that none of these examples involves a written test; yet you would know immediately whether your learners "got it" or not. Academic rigor, active learning, authentic outcomes, and alternative approaches are all shown here.

Here are some more ideas:

- Ask students to construct a product such as a game or test that would assess the learning with someone else.
- Guide learners in assembling a portfolio containing various products that highlight the academic expectations.
- Give open-book tests.
- Give learners the test questions in advance of the test.
- Give take-home tests with clear instructions.
- Give partner or group tests.
- Ask learners to write the test questions; then use the questions by passing them around the class for other learners to answer.

Showcase Achievement

The final *A* is to recognize and reward achievement with your class, both as individuals and as a group. The most effective way for you to motivate your learners to tackle future challenges is for you to reinforce their successes with current tasks. You want to celebrate each accomplishment and help your students make the critical connections to their own learning and independence. You want to maintain a positive and productive outlook so your learners believe that you share in their successes.

Achievement includes the process and the product. That means you want to involve the students in the selection and direction not only of their learning, but of their attitudes and approaches toward assessment. You want to make clear and model how planning one's learning, conducting one's learning, and demonstrating one's learning makes an individual feel good. Success builds success. Take on a group "can do" spirit; join your learners as if you were one of them. When you need to correct or redirect your learners, stay calm and showcase their achievements, too.

Your learners will connect with you more if they think you like and respect them. They need to internalize that they have a chance to succeed with you and at all times. If you allow a student to give up, it will require a huge amount of effort to help him or her reinvest in you, themselves, and the learning. *How* you conduct your summative assessments must be considered in partnership with *what* you include on your summative assessments.

Continue the Assessment Cycle . . .

Assessment is nonstop. It is integral from preparation and facilitation through reflection and modification. It is vital to fully understand your learners, your teaching, and the schooling. Acquiring an assessment mindset that is positive and productive will change your approaches, so you start with your assessments.

Extend With Questions and Activities

Frequently Asked Questions

1. How do I know which summative assessments are best?

Keep the five *A*s in mind: academic rigor, active learning, authentic outcomes, alternative choices, and learner achievement. As you develop a variety of assessments to collect preassessment, formative, and summative assessment data, you will rapidly realize which ones fit best into your repertoire. Here are insights from one eighth-grade teacher:

> *The list of learning expectations is huge, and I have to be sure that everyone is as ready as possible for the next grade. Our units last about three weeks; that's when I conduct the summative assessments. I have developed three versions of summative assessments that I use most of the time. I rotate through the three assessments in a way that prior learning becomes part of the new learning.*

2. How can I involve my learners when collecting summative data?

As you construct your summative assessment checklists and rubrics, include a column or space for your learners to reflect on their progress and report their outcomes. Show the assessment tool to your learners when you assign instruction. Your learners will be thrilled to be part of the entire procedure, and, usually, they score themselves lower than you do. You will want to guide your learners through their own self-assessments.

3. Where can I get more ideas for summative assessments?

Talk with the learners and your colleagues, look in the teaching guides, surf the Internet, and let your imagination guide you. Develop your summative assessments so that they showcase the expectations in ways that are natural and connect with the real world. Check out the list of Web sites in Appendix D.

Activities

1. Using one of your learning experiences, select a common manipulative for your learners to demonstrate to you a summative assessment.

2. Write three different summative performance-based assessments you can use for a favorite unit of learning.

3. Show your learners how you want them to demonstrate their learning to you at the end of the first learning experience in a unit of learning.

4. Tell a colleague about a successful summative assessment that you implemented in your classroom today.

5. Start a record-keeping system to become aware of your current approaches to summative assessments in your classroom.

7

Identifying
What to Assess

Inviting the Five Types
of Inquiry and Information

Conversations about performance-based assessments revolve around three major questions: *when* to assess, *what* to assess, and *how* to assess effectively and efficiently. Chapters 3, 4, 5, and 6 detailed when to assess (before, during, and after the learning and teaching). To guide the conversations addressing what to assess, this chapter describes the five types of inquiry and information that you must introduce to your learners to elicit the thinking, engagement, and responses that you hope to ignite in your teaching.

Introduce the Five Types of Inquiry

During all your assessments, you ask questions and assign tasks to prompt various levels of thinking and combinations of expectations across your content subject areas. There are times that you want your learners to give a quick one-word or single response; there are times that you want them to expand upon a response or to give the steps for solving a problem. And then there are times that you want your learners to construct an original story, to create and build a project, or to make a presentation to the class. But before you can plan *how* you are going to assess your learners (that is, apply the forms of appraisal and authentication), you must determine *what* you are going to assess (that is, identify the types of inquiries and information that you are seeking).

These five types of inquiry and information can help you invite your learners to exhibit their performance-based assessments in all subject areas:

1. Recognition and recall

2. Logic and reasoning

3. Skills and applications

4. Productivity and creativity

5. Outlooks and dispositions

The five types of inquiry and information are extended from the research of Stiggins (2007). You may recognize the levels of questions from the taxonomies of Bloom and Marzano (see Appendix B).

However, unlike Bloom and Marzano, the five types of inquiry and information should not be viewed as hierarchies, with one type of inquiry and information more or less complex than the other types of inquiries and information. Each type of inquiry and information presented in this chapter should be used to elicit a different type of outcome and for a different reason. You want all students to strengthen their learning (your teaching, and the schooling) in every way possible. Table 7.1 lists the five types of inquiry and information with prompts.

Remember: Performance-based assessments are much more than just tests at the end of a learning experience or unit of learning. Every formal and informal interaction, both planned and spontaneous, that you conduct with your learners contributes to your assessments of your students as individuals, as members of groups, and as a whole class. Learning incorporates a balance of immediate recognition of information (II), continuous development of essential concepts (CC), and unending lifelong understandings (UU) as discussed in Chapter 4. Class conversations, oral reading, board work, group charts, worksheets, pictures, diagrams, and journal writing are all performance-based assessments that can be used as preassessments, formative assessments, and summative assessments.

Table 7.1 Five Types of Inquiry and Information With Prompts

Type of Inquiry and Information	Prompt
1. Recognition and recall	Who, What, Where, and When
2. Logic and reasoning	Why, Why not, and Explain
3. Skills and applications	How, Point to, and Show me the steps
4. Productivity and creativity	How else, What other way, and What else might happen
5. Outlooks and dispositions	How do you feel, How does someone feel, and How might you feel if

SOURCE: Adapted from Stiggins (2007).

Rely Upon Recognition and Recall

Recognition and recall of information asks questions or assigns tasks, probing declarative knowledge starting with "Who," "What," "Where," and "When." Although you may view these prompts as simpler questions than the prompts associated with other types of inquiry and information, these words may be quite difficult for some learners and can become challenging depending on the context. Context is defined by your students (the learning), your purpose (the teaching), and your situation (the schooling). You always want to connect the context to your choice of performance-based assessments.

Recognition of knowledge includes acknowledging, detecting, and identifying information by the learner. Here are some examples stimulating recognition, using different prompts to start the question:

- *Who do you see in the picture?*
- *What is Step 2 in the process?*
- *Where did you find the title of the book?*
- *When do we go to lunch?*

Recall of knowledge entails remembering, evoking, and recollecting information by the learner. Here are some examples that investigate recall using each of the four prompts:

- *Who was the first U.S. president?*
- *What was the reason for the accident?*
- *Where did we go on our field trip yesterday?*
- *When was the school festival held?*

Promote Logic and Reasoning

The second type of inquiry and information promotes logic and reasoning; this type asks questions or assigns tasks, probing conditional knowledge starting with "Why," "Why not," and "Explain." As you can see, this type of inquiry and information asks different kinds of questions and poses different kinds of prompts than posed with recognition and recall. Although logic and reasoning questions tend to be more difficult and challenging than recognition and recall, again, please note that the five types of inquiry and information incorporated in performance-based assessments are not placed in a hierarchy of higher-order thinking. Each type of inquiry and information plays an important role in assessing conversations, assignments, and examinations. Frequently, when asking questions or assigning tasks related to logic and reasoning, you must start with or incorporate questions or tasks related to recognition and recall.

Logic involves explanation, motivation, judgment, and wisdom by the learner. You want your students to give you a rationale, make a decision, and/or connect personal insights with the learning. Here are some examples that promote logic:

- *Why did the woman take that action?*
- *Why didn't the voters pass the law?*
- *Explain our system to the new student and why we like it.*

Reasoning entails analysis, calculation, estimation, and interpretation by the learner. You want your students to inspect the information or steps, predict an outcome, and/or give a different version accounting for the cause and/or effects. Here are some examples that examine reasoning:

- *Why do think the experiment worked this time?*
- *Why aren't the children going on the field trip?*
- *Explain the steps we followed in making that decision.*

Analyze Skills and Applications

This third type of inquiry and information asks questions and assigns tasks by *examining students' abilities to do things, probing both procedural knowledge and application knowledge, starting with "How," "Point to," and "Show me."*

Skills involve processes or expertise to demonstrate learning, illustrate required components or steps, and fulfill a charge. Everything you teach involves skills. Reading, writing, speaking, listening, viewing, spelling, and identifying grammar are all skills. Calculating mentally, on paper, on the board, or on a calculator or with a computer involve skills. Demonstrating a science experiment or presenting a science project, drawing a map or creating a chart about government, all of these are skills. Many important skills are taught in today's classrooms as individual skills, combined skills, and background skills necessary to answer more complex questions or to complete more advanced tasks.

Here are some examples that analyze skills:

- *Read the passage that explains the cause of the problem.*
- *Circle the capital of the country on the map.*
- *Calculate the solution to this math problem.*

Applications differ from skills in that the learner must transfer the learning to new and perhaps unknown contexts. Applications demonstrate the use, purpose, and relevance in ways for which the student may or may not have been prepared.

Here are some examples that call for applications:

- *Tell me how to find a book in a library that you have never visited.*
- *Point to the new words that have the same pattern as we studied yesterday.*
- *Show me what happens when we combine the two steps in a different situation.*

Demonstrate Productivity and Creativity

A fourth type of inquiry and information promotes *productivity and creativity by asking questions or assigning tasks that probe problem-solving knowledge, starting with "How else," "What other way," and "What else might happen."*

Productivity involves doing, making, and constructing. Here are some examples that showcase productivity:

- *How else can you read the chart?*
- *What other way can you write that sentence?*
- *What else might happen if you add another weight to the balance?*

Creativity involves originality, imagination, and resourcefulness. Here are some examples that motivate creativity:

- *How else can you solve that math problem?*
- *What other way can you express your ideas?*
- *What else might happen if you include another person in the project?*

Probe Outlooks and Dispositions

The fifth type of inquiry and information discussed in this chapter promotes dispositions and outlooks, asking questions or assigns tasks that probe critical thinking and evaluation knowledge, starting with "How do you feel," "How does someone feel," and "How might you feel if."

Outlooks involve attitudes, viewpoints, and perspectives. Here are some examples that explore outlooks:

- *How do you feel when your paper is published in the newsletter?*
- *How does an inventor feel when the invention is popular?*
- *How might you feel if you had shared your idea in class and people didn't like it?*

Dispositions involve personality, character, and temperament. Outlooks and dispositions are similar, and you may see them as being synonymous. Outlooks pertain more to attitudes and viewpoints that are expressed outwardly and can be modified. Dispositions are characteristics that are more internal and are less easily modified. Here are some examples that delve into dispositions:

- *How do you feel when there is a substitute teacher?*
- *How does someone feel if they get to be the leader?*
- *How might you feel if you lost your part of the group project?*

Tables 7.2 through 7.5 offer classroom prompts and examples of the five types of inquiry in four content subject areas: literacy, math, science, and social studies.

Balance Three Conditions
With Five Types of Inquiry

All five types of inquiry and information are influenced by three important conditions. The questions that you ask and the tasks that you assign will range from:

1. Simple to complex

2. Concrete to abstract

3. Single viewpoint to multiple perspectives

Let's examine each of these three ranges of conditions as scales. You will want to use all three at different times with different students

(Text continues on page 142)

Table 7.2 Inquiry and Information—Literacy: Fictional Story

Type of Inquiry and Information	Prompt	Inquiries for Fictional Story
1. Recognition and recall	Who, What, Where, and When	• Who is the main character? • What is this character's name? • Where does this story take place? • When does this story take place?
2. Logic and reasoning	Why, Why not, and Explain	• Why did the main character take the trip? • Why did the main character not travel another day? • Explain what you predict the main character intends to do while on the trip.
3. Skills and applications	How, Point to, and Show me how/the steps	• How do know what will happen? • Point to a description passage in the story that tells how the main character feels during the trip. • Show me a timeline of events in the story.
4. Productivity and creativity	How else, What other way, and What else might happen	• How else could the main character get into trouble? • What other way could the main character solve the problem faster? • What else do you predict could happen in this story?
5. Outlooks and dispositions	How do you feel, How does a person feel, and How might you feel if	• How do you feel about the main character? • How do most people feel about this situation? • How might you feel if this happened to you?

Table 7.3 Inquiry and Information—Math: Subtraction

Type of Inquiry and Information	Prompt	Inquiries for Subtraction
1. Recognition and recall	Who, What, Where, and When	• Who has a math problem where you need to borrow? • What is the solution? • Where do you borrow a number? • When do you borrow a number?

(Continued)

Table 7.3 (Continued)

Type of Inquiry and Information	Prompt	Inquiries for Subtraction
2. Logic and reasoning	*Why, Why not, and Explain*	• Why do you have to borrow in this problem? • Why do you not have to borrow in this problem? • Explain how to subject.
3. Skills and applications	*How, Point to, and Show me how/the steps*	• How do you subtract and borrow in your head (doing mental math)? • Point to a math problem where you do not need to borrow to subtract. • Show me how to borrow.
4. Productivity and creativity	*How else, What other way, and What else might happen*	• How else do you need to do to solve this math problem? • What other way can you solve this math problem? • What else might you want to know to solve this math problem?
5. Outlooks and dispositions	*How do you feel, How does a person feel, and How might you feel if*	• How do you feel about subtracting and borrowing? • How does our class feel now about subtracting and borrowing? • How might you feel if you could borrow in your head more often?

Table 7.4   Inquiry and Information—Science: Pets/Animals

Type of Inquiry and Information	Prompt	Inquiries for Pets/Animals
1. Recognition and recall	*Who, What, Where, and When*	• Who has a pet and/or animal at home? • What is your pet and/or animal? • Where do you keep your pet and/or animal? • When do you feed your pet and/or animal?

Type of Inquiry and Information	Prompt	Inquiries for Pets/Animals
2. Logic and reasoning	*Why, Why not, and Explain*	• Why do you have this kind of pet and/or animal? • Why did you not get a different kind of pet and/or animal? • Explain how your pet and/or animal is important to you.
3. Skills and applications	*How, Point to, and Show me how/the steps*	• How do you care for your pet and/or animal? • Point to a picture of your pet and/or animal. • Show me how you feed your pet and/or animal.
4. Productivity and creativity	*How else, What other way, and What else might happen*	• How else might you care for your pet and/or animal? • Draw me a picture of another way to care for your pet and/or animal. • What might happen if you did not care for your pet and/or animal?
5. Outlooks and dispositions	*How do you feel, How does a person feel, and How might you feel if*	• How do you feel about your pet and/or animal? • How does your family feel about your pet and/or animal? • How might you feel if you lost your pet and/or animal?

Table 7.5   Inquiry and Information—Social Studies: Our State

Type of Inquiry and Information	Prompt	Inquiries for Our State
1. Recognition and recall	*Who, What, Where, and When*	• Who is the governor? • What is the state capital? • Where is the state capital? • When is the state birthday?

(Continued)

Table 7.5 (Continued)

Type of Inquiry and Information	Prompt	Inquiries for Our State
2. Logic and reasoning	*Why, Why not, and Explain*	• Why do we have a governor? • Why does the state not have a president? • Explain how we elect the governor of our state.
3. Skills and applications	*How, Point to, and Show me how/the steps*	• How do laws get passed in our state? • Point to the illustration showing how a bill becomes a law. • Show me how we find official information about our state.
4. Productivity and creativity	*How else, What other way, and What else might happen*	• How else might you find information about our state? • What other way can a bill become a law? • What might happen if you break a law?
5. Outlooks and dispositions	*How do you feel, How does a person feel, and How might you feel if*	• How do you feel about our state? • How does your family feel about our state? • How might you feel if you could travel to any place you want in our state?

for different reasons. And all three scales will be evident in every single conversation, assignment, and assessment.

1. *Simple to complex.* A simple question or task is one that appears to have only one straightforward or seemingly right answer. A complex question or task is more intricate or complicated and can be answered with many different answers. For this scale, not only is there a wide range of unique qualities spanning simple to complex, but the scale will differ for each learner depending on individual achievement levels. You want to be ready to delve in ways that are developmentally appropriate with your learners to challenge and stimulate their thinking individually and as a whole class.

2. *Concrete to abstract.* A concrete question or task is one that elicits a real or physical example; it seems to be well known and

commonly accepted. An abstract question or task is one that is conceptual and intangible. Again, you want to consider the wide range of possibilities on this scale as you introduce a topic and expand students' thinking. You may want to review thinking in Chapter 4 to become more familiar with inductive and deductive as well as convergent and divergent thinking.

3. *Single viewpoint to multiple viewpoint.* A single viewpoint tends to belongs to only one individual; multiple perspectives relate to many different people's viewpoints or perceptions. The range of responses that you can draw out of your learners related to their individual ideas and supporting examples will make your classroom much more alive and dynamic. This scale is one of the most exciting, as you empower your learners to jump in to express their beliefs and opinions. When you open your class conversations to include viewpoints, you are creating a community of learners in a shared environment that will be extremely beneficial and rewarding for everyone.

Each of these scales of consideration can be illustrated with questions based on "Who." When you ask a student, "Who is the main character in the story?" the response may be the one you are seeking (the response you consider to be the correct answer), or the student may tell you the character that they believe is the main character for a different, more complex reason.

Recognition and recall also involves concrete and abstract thinking. You might ask a student, "Who won the race?" You expect the student to tell you the name of the person who came in first place. However, your student may give you a different response based on different criteria.

Additionally, recognition and recall involves multiple viewpoints and diverse perspectives in one's thinking. You might ask a learner, "Who is your grandfather?" Your learner may or may not know the grandfather's name, other than the family name the grandchildren have always used. You have to determine if this answer is correct or sufficient.

You must frame your questions and prompts carefully to elicit the answers you are seeking, or you must be ready to accept the answers you are given. Be aware that you might announce that the answer is not correct, when, indeed, the answer is correct according to a different source. You want to model mindfulness in your interactions with learners so they will participate willingly in all performance-based assessments. Be careful not to step on learners' confidence when you are seeking a specific answer to a question. That game is known as "Guess what the teacher is thinking," and you are encouraged to avoid it altogether.

Delve Into Responses

When implementing your questions and tasks, it is essential to delve into your students' responses. This means you must be ready to ask appropriate follow-up questions during in-class discussions; probe a little further during individual assistance; ask students to describe, justify, give the significance, explain what they did, or tell how they feel about a product or process. All of these interactions constitute delving.

Delving does not come easily to many teachers, especially novice teachers. From a first-year teacher:

> *I wasn't sure how to ask questions when I began teaching. Most of my questions were rather basic so I could keep everyone on task and keep moving. I think I was afraid of asking questions that I wouldn't know if the answers were correct. I was also fearful that the class would get out of control if we started a discussion not directly related to the topic.*

Many teachers are, first, overjoyed that the student produced the correct response, and, second, are not prepared to advance the conversation. Many teachers rely upon the questions in the textbook or use questions that come to their minds during the teaching. Lack of preparation certainly is not going to help you delve. You are highly encouraged to be ready to delve; try to prepare a few questions related to all five types of inquiry and information.

Another concern relates to teachers' practices when delving. There is a tendency for teachers to delve more with students who probably know the answers than with students who probably do not know the answers. The tendency also is for teachers to delve with boys than with girls (Sadker & Sadker, 1994) and to delve more with white students than students of color (Ladson-Billings, 1995). You want to be careful that you delve in ways that help all of your learners to shine and avoid delving in ways that can embarrass or humiliate learners.

From a veteran teacher:

> *At first, I asked the harder questions of the stronger students. Naturally, their learning advanced more quickly. I was thinking that everyone was learning. Sometimes I would ask students questions when they were not paying attention to try to bring them back to the discussion. Neither one of these approaches is helpful.*

As you grow in your teaching, most likely you will become more adept at delving. Here are some examples of delving related to recognition and recall:

- *Who is a good source to help you with your task?*
- *What is not being stated in this speech?*
- *Where is the second largest continent?*
- *When do you imagine the mystery will be solved?*

Related to logic and reasoning:

- *Why does this computation solve the word problem?*
- *Why did you not use these blocks in your construction?*
- *Explain when and how you knew the outcome of the story.*

Related to skills and applications:

- *How can you make that work faster?*
- *Point to the location where the two lines cross.*
- *Show me the way that your friend showed you.*

Related to productivity and creativity:

- *How else can your friend edit the paper?*
- *What other way might solve the problem using fewer steps?*
- *What else might happen if the water overflows?*

Related to outlooks and dispositions:

- *How do you feel when your pet is injured?*
- *How might you feel if that disaster happened to your family?*
- *How might you feel if you were suddenly a different person?*

Enhance Variety in Your Inquiries

All five types of inquiry and information will help you vary your teaching strategies and learning experiences with your students to promote motivation, engagement, and achievement. As you incorporate every type of inquiry and information in your performance-based assessments, your learners will grow and develop holistically.

They will see and connect prior knowledge and experiences with new expectations and outcomes. Your learners will view feedback as positive and productive processes that fortify rather than undermine their academic progress. Transfer of learning will increase and strengthen students' achievement when you integrate all five types of inquiry and information across the curriculum. Ultimately, you want your students to understand that learning is an individual process; the more they can look at their own learning in context, the more they will take responsibility for their learning.

Include All Types of Thinking, Acting, and Feeling . . .

Learning balances the head, the hands, and the heart, visible through the acquisition, application, and appreciation of new and expanded awareness and comprehension. Your goals are to investigate the five types of inquiries and information with every learner every day to build continuous concepts and strengthen unending understandings.

Chapter 8 addresses how to apply the five forms of appraisal and authentication (*what* and *how* to assess), showing you how to activate and analyze the various techniques you can use in your preassessments, formative assessments, and summative assessments. In Chapter 9, you combine the five types of inquiry and information and the five forms of appraisal into a practical and easy-to-use template for planning, aligning, preparing, facilitating, analyzing, and reflecting on your performance-based assessments.

Extend With Questions and Activities

Frequently Asked Questions

1. **What can I do to prepare using all five types of inquiry and information with my assessments?**

Begin by taking one of your favorite learning experiences and writing some questions for each of the five types of inquiry and information. Look at the examples in Tables 7.2 through 7.5.

2. **How can I know which types of inquiry and information my learners prefer?**

When you are asking questions in class or giving assignments, watch and listen as your learners interact in the discussions and react to the tasks. Also, ask your learners directly to tell you which questions and tasks are easiest to answer or complete. Ask them to explain their answers, too. They will enjoy giving you feedback.

3. Why is it important for me to use all five types of inquiry and information?

Although you have identified questions to prompt all five types of inquiry and information and you know your learners' favorite types, most likely you have a tendency to use the types of inquiry and information that you prefer using the most. Every teacher has this tendency. If you use the chart to guide you, you'll be sure to include all five types of inquiry and information. Then your teaching and your learners' learning will be well-rounded and balanced.

Activities

1. Select an upcoming learning experience and write one example of the five types of inquiries and information to use immediately and practice your new expertise.

2. After using your five new inquiries and information, compare and contrast this learning experience with previous learning experiences.

3. During a learning experience in which you want your learners to ask questions, show them the five types of inquiries and ask them to craft questions using all five types.

4. Practice using all five types of inquiries and information by adding more learning experiences in one subject area and then expanding to more subject areas.

5. Identify the subject areas where your competence and confidence are stronger for incorporating all five types of inquiries and information. Analyze the success and reward you find in this subject area and consider how you can transfer the success to other subject areas. You can share your observations with your mentor.

8

Analyzing
How to Assess

Applying the Five Forms
of Appraisal and Authentication

The five forms of appraisal and authentication are going to change your professional efficacy and, more important, your learners' success. As you check the learning during preassessments, formative assessments, and summative assessments, you are appraising all of your goals: *as* learning, *for* learning, and *of* learning. Imagine when a piece of property is appraised. The appraiser checks the property *as* a solid structure, *for* your insured investment, and *of* its overall worth. These three goals are essential to the owner *as* a home, *for* future resale, and to be a viable part *of* the community. The appraiser also assesses the property in ways that are both criterion referenced (compared and contrasted with a list of standard expectations) and norm referenced (compared and contrasted with other similar homes in the area).

The property analogy fits perfectly with your professional practices. Your assessments must be sound, valuable, and worthy of everyone's time, money, and energy. All five forms of appraisal and authentication can be used before, during, and after the learning through formal and informal interactions. Try to use all five forms in every class every day. You, your learners, and their families will be quite impressed how your transformed assessments change your learning environment.

Analyze the Five Forms of Appraisal and Authentication

The word *appraise* means to review and decide. That is precisely what you do using the five forms of appraisal. The evidence is examined and a decision is made. Assessments can be conducted by you (the teacher), by the students themselves, by students' peers, students' families, and outsiders. Appraisals may be decided by one person or by many people working collaboratively or alone.

The word *authenticate* means to confirm and substantiate. You want to confirm that your assessments elicit outcomes that verify that learning has occurred and in the most natural and real situation possible.

All assessments fit into one of the five forms of appraisal and authentication:

1. Selected answers

2. Written responses

3. Demonstrated performances

4. Spoken communications

5. Combined forms

By combining the five types of appraisal and authentication into groups of two, three, and four types of appraisals, you have eleven different choices to use in your assessments. For example, you can combine selected answers with written responses, or you could merge demonstrated performances with spoken communications. The five types of appraisal, including the eleven choices for combined forms, are presented with prompts and applications in Table 8.1.

Pick Selected Answers

The form of selected answers is the easiest and most commonly used form of appraisal. It involves the learner choosing an answer from a given selection or from a provided list. Selected answers may feature more

(Text continues on page 155)

Table 8.1 Five Types of Appraisal and Authentication With Prompts and Applications

Selected Answers *Prompt: Pick*

Matching
Multiple choice
True/false
From a word list:
  • Fill-in-the-blank
  • Categorize
  • Group
  • Label

Written Responses *Prompt: Write*

One letter	Directions
One word	Drawings
One phrase	Editorials
One sentence	E-mail messages
Several sentences	Epilogues
Paragraph	Essays:
Short story	• Cause/effect
Long story	• Comparison/contrast
Report	• Personal
In any and all contexts of writing:	• Persuasion
Agendas	• Reaction
Anecdote	• Reflection
Argument	• Response
Autobiographies	Examinations
Bibliographies	Fictional narratives:
Biographies	• Fables
Bumper stickers	• Fairy tales
Business letters	• Mysteries
Captions	• Novellas
Cartoons	• Romance
Charts	• Short stories
Content area logs	• Tall tales
Content area observations	Field notes
Contracts	Flowcharts
Critiques	Fortunes
Data sheets	Free writing
Descriptions	Friendly letters
Dialogue	Graffiti
Diaries	Graphic organizers
Dictation	

(Continued)

Table 8.1 (Continued)

Graphs
How-to-do papers
Illustrations
Indexes/indices
Instructions
Interviews
Invitations
Jokes and riddles
Journals
Letters of:
- Application
- Appreciation
- Congratulations
- Sympathy

Lab reports
Lists
Literary analyses
Logs
Magazine articles
Memoirs
Memos
Menus
Mottoes and slogans
Multiple perspectives
Myths
News
Newspaper articles
Notes
Nursery rhymes
Observations
Parodies
Personal essays
Personal journals
Personal narratives
Picture books
Plays
Poetry
Political statements
Postcards
PowerPoint slides

Prefaces
Profiles/portraits
Public notices:
- Advertisements
- Announcement
- Fliers
- Posters

Recipes
Reports
Research papers
Résumés
Reviews
Scripts:
- Plays
- Puppet shows
- Radio plays
- Skits
- Speeches
- Television commercials
- Television shows

Sketches
Songs and raps
Stories
Tables of contents
Telegrams
Timelines
Weather reports

In ways that are
- Applied
- Clarifying
- Conditional
- Creative
- Declarative
- Documented
- Expository
- Personal
- Philosophic
- Problem solving
- Procedural
- Provocative
- Technical

Demonstrated Performances
Prompt: Show

Act	Locate
Calculations	Model
Dance	Parade
Demonstrate	Perform
Direct	Point
Display	Portrayals
Exemplify	Present
Exhibit	Reveal
Find	Role playing
Games	Show
Guide	Simulations
Lead	Steps of a process

Spoken Communications
Prompt: Say

Conferences	Oral reports
Discussions, small group	Presentations, class
Discussions, whole class	Presentations, individual
Interviews	Presentations, small group
Oral exams	Telephone calls
Oral readings	

Combined Forms of Appraisals
Prompts: 11 Possibilities

• *Pick and write*	• *Pick, write, and show*
• *Pick and show*	• *Pick, write, and say*
• *Pick and say*	• *Pick, show, and say*
• *Write and show*	• *Write, show, and say*
• *Write and say*	• *Pick, write, show, and say*
• *Say and show*	

Author's chair	Coins
Brainstorming	Collections
Brain teasers	Committees
Bulletin boards	Computers
Buzz groups	Conferences
Captions	Cooking
Cartoons	Critical thinking
Case studies	Crosswords
Chalkboard activities	Current events
Charts	Dances
Choral speaking	Debates

(Continued)

Table 8.1 (Continued)

Deductive strategies	Panels
Demonstrations	Pen pals
Diaries	Photographs
Dioramas	Pictures
Discussions	Plays
Dolls	Posters
Dramatics	Problem solving
Experiments	Puppets
Field trips	Puzzles
Films	Questioning
Flags	Questions
Flannel boards	Quizzes
Flash cards	Readers' theater
Flowcharts	Reading
Games	Records
Globes	Reference materials
Goal setting	Reports
Graphs	Reproductions
Guest speaker interviews	Role playing
Halls of fame	Sand tables
Hobbies	School events
Homework	Scientific methods
Inductive strategies	Scrapbooks
Inquiry	Service projects
Integration	Sewing
Interviews	Simulations
Jigsaw strategies	Slides
Journals	Stamps
Letter writing	Story telling
Listening	Surveys
Magazines	Talks
Maps	Tapes
Media	Technology
Mentoring	Television
Mobiles	Tests
Mock trials	Textbooks
Modeling	Think-Pair-Share
Models	Timelines
Montages	Trips
Murals	Videos
Music	Visualizing
Newspapers	Webbing
Notebooks	Word games/associations
Openers	

SOURCE: Adapted from Stiggins (2007).

recognition and recall than other types of inquiry and information. The key word to remember for selected answers is *pick*. When appraising with selected answers, the assessment coordinates with the type of inquiry or information. Table 8.2 shows suggestions for constructing selected answers assessment items.

Selected answers assessments can be constructed in many different ways to fit the learning outcomes and teaching needs. Multiple choice items work well to assess concepts and big ideas. When using multiple choice statements, you can include two or more choices. You

Table 8.2   Constructing Selected Answers Assessment Items

---

1. Keep items short by writing them on one line as often as possible.

2. Each item should assess only one expectation; avoid overcomplicating the assessment by using double answers (*a* and *c*), *all of the above,* or *none of the above.*

3. Items should be written clearly and without ambiguity, with one correct answer selected from five choices; incorrect answers are called *reasonable distracters.*

4. Distribute items for matching, multiple choice, fill-in-the blank, and so forth, logically.

5. Select a balanced number of items for matching, multiple choice, fill-in-the blank, and so forth.

6. Place items in a logical order.

7. Write items that seek five types of inquiry and information, especially concepts, and include charts, graphs, maps, and other visuals.

8. Use developmentally appropriate vocabulary reading levels.

9. Avoid giving clues in the question or statement stem.

10. Include clear directions for each item and each section of the assessment.

11. Place all items for a section on one side of the paper.

12. For matching: Place choices in a column on the right; include more choices than needed.

13. For multiple choice: Limit choices to three words or phrases.

14. For true/false: Be absolutely sure of the statement and avoid double negatives.

15. For fill-in-the-blank: Be clear whether choices can be used only one time or more than one time.

also can include selected answers with combinations of choices, for example, "Answers a *and* b," "All the above," and "None of the above." Matching assessments are super for vocabulary and links between categories, for example, individuals and inventions. Assessments featuring fill-in-the-blank from a list allows learners to make connections that range from concrete to abstract. True/false tend to be more appropriate for clear-cut information and practices.

The advantages of selected answers include the ease of grouping large amounts of information together quickly. The appraisal item can be lifted directly from the textbook and glossary for both teacher and learner convenience. With proper planning and item construction, all types of inquiry and information, from small detailed factual recall to big ideas and concepts, can be assessed using selected answers. Some selected answer assessment items are easy to write; all of them are easy to score and to score objectively, particularly as you do not have to read the students' handwriting. You can diagnose difficulties from repeated error patterns.

The disadvantages of selected answers are the assessment items may be difficult to write and take more time than you anticipate. Writing questions and statements with developmental language levels that all learners can read and understand can be challenging. Writing true/false statements that are clearly true or false is complicated.

Teachers tend to use similar patterns when writing assessments with selected answers, and students may concentrate more on detecting the pattern than picking the best answer. Students can guess at the correct answers, and they do not show any work through which you can follow their thinking. Students' guessing limits your ability to detect learning patterns.

Table 8.3 presents suggested instructions for selected answers form of appraisal for each of the five types of inquiry and information.

Use Written Responses

Written responses are recorded through various styles of writing generated by the learner. The key word to remember for written responses is *write*. Written responses include fill-in-the-blank statements (from no list), short answer questions or stem completions, answers to questions, or fulfillments of prompts. Table 8.4 presents suggestions for constructing written response assessment items.

Each of the suggestions for constructing written response assessment items may be placed in any and all contexts that relate to your grade level, subject area, and unit of learning. Written responses

Table 8.3   Selected Answers Suggestions for the Five Types of Inquiry and Information

Type of Inquiry and Information	Selected Answers Prompts	Selected Answers Suggestions
1. Recognition and recall	Who, What, Where, and When	• *Who:* Match the individual with the place. • *What:* Pick the item to finish the statement. • *Where:* Circle each correctly labeled river. • *When:* Use the list to complete the timeline.
2. Logic and reasoning	Why, Why not, and Explain	• *Why:* Draw a line from the item to the reason. • *Why not:* Circle the one word in each category that does not fit with the heading. • *Explain:* Underline the one response that best describes the situation.
3. Skills and applications	How, Point to, and Show me how/the steps	• *How:* Match the phrase on the right with the phrase on the left explaining how to solve the math problem. • *Point to:* Point to the word that fills in the labels. • *Show me the steps:* Place a check mark next to the three signs that identify the three steps for conducting the experiment.
4. Productivity and creativity	How else, What other way, and What else might happen	• *How else:* Draw a line from the beginning of the sentence to the end of the sentence that shows how else we can write the sentence. • *What other way:* Place a star next to one phrase from the list to add to each category. • *What else might happen:* Mark A, B, C, or D as to what else might happen logically in the story.
5. Outlooks and dispositions	How do you feel, How does some one feel, and How might you feel if	• *How do you feel:* Circle the icon that shows how you feel at the end of the race. • *How does someone feel:* Draw a line from the individual's name to the phrase to match the people with their feelings. • *How might you feel if:* Highlight the label in the list that describes how you might feel in each situation.

Table 8.4   Constructing Written Responses Assessment Items

1. Keep items short by writing them on one line as often as possible.

2. Each item should assess only one expectation; don't overcomplicate the assessment.

3. Items should be written clearly and without ambiguity, with one correct response.

4. Distribute items for various kinds of written responses logically with other forms of appraisals.

5. Select a limited number of items for short answer and written responses; closely monitor the total time needed to complete the assessment.

6. Place items in a logical order.

7. Write items that seek all five types of inquiry and information.

8. Use developmentally appropriate vocabulary and reading levels.

9. Avoid giving clues in the question or statement stem.

10. Include clear directions for each item and each section of the assessment.

11. Leave space to write the response on the same side of the paper with the question.

12. For short answer: Ask for only one example in the response.

13. For written responses: Ask for the specific number of examples.

14. For written responses: Stipulate how the written content and writing mechanisms will be scored.

15. For written responses: Ask questions that seek explanations and examples; avoid written responses that require recitation of memorized information.

encompass endless opportunities, such as those listed in Table 5.3 in Chapter 5. From your daily interactions with your learners, you can gain all sorts of creative and challenging ideas. Talk with your colleagues, too. Let your imagination be your guide.

The advantage of written responses is that they allow you to appraise a broad range of thinking that is original and creative, covering many types of inquiry and information. Students cannot guess unless clues can be found in the item or in other items found on the assessment. You can diagnose different kinds of errors on written response items.

The disadvantages of written responses reveal that they are time consuming to prepare fairly and with samples for each anticipated level of outcome. And they require much longer to score. Scoring written responses involves reading for content and mechanics. Depending on the type of inquiry or information, the written response may be more advanced and complex; scoring can become more subjective.

Table 8.5 presents suggested instructions for the written responses form of appraisal for each of the five types of inquiry and information.

Table 8.5 Written Response Suggestions for the Five Types of Inquiry and Information

Type of Inquiry and Information	Written Response Prompts	Written Response Suggestions
1. Recognition and recall	Who, What, Where, and When	• *Who:* Who invented the ice cream cone? • *What:* What is the woman wearing on her head? • *Where:* Where is the Nile River? • *When:* When does the music begin?
2. Logic and reasoning	Why, Why not, and Explain	• *Why:* Why does the boy bring his friend with him to the party? • *Why not:* Why can you not use that number to solve the problem? • *Explain:* Explain the difference between a gas and a liquid.
3. Skills and applications	How, Point to, and Show me the steps	• *How:* Describe in one paragraph how we predict the weather. • *Point to:* Point to the letters that identify the plurals for each word. • *Show me the steps:* Show me how to write the sentence correctly.
4. Productivity and creativity	How else, What other way, and What else might happen	• *How else:* Finish the sentence identifying how else we could make a decision. • *What other way:* In your report, tell another way the children could get home. • *What else might happen:* Write a new caption to the picture describing what else might happen if the dog sneaks into the school.
5. Outlooks and dispositions	How do you feel, How does someone feel, and How might you feel if	• *How do you feel:* Write one word for how you feel today. • *How does someone feel:* Add words to the song describing how the family feels. • *How might you feel if:* Write three phrases for how you might feel if the town were to get a new recreation center.

Show Demonstrated Performances

Demonstrated performances are created by and presented through physical motion. Table 8.6 presents suggestions for constructing demonstrated performance assessment items.

Table 8.7 models suggested instructions for the demonstrated performance form of appraisal for each of the five types of inquiry and information.

The advantages of demonstrated performances emphasize opportunities for learners to show not only what they know but how they constructed the knowledge or skills to solve a problem. The teacher can watch the student closely to appraise each step in the learning

Table 8.6   Constructing Demonstrated Performance Assessment Items

1. Keep items short so they are spoken briefly.

2. Each item should assess only one expectation; don't overcomplicate the assessment.

3. Items should be demonstrated clearly and without ambiguity, with one correct response.

4. Distribute items for various kinds of demonstrated performances logically with other forms of appraisals.

5. Select a limited number of items to demonstrate performances; closely monitor the total time needed to complete the assessment.

6. Place items in a logical order.

7. Ask or write items that seek all five types of inquiry and information.

8. Use developmentally appropriate vocabulary for speaking and reading levels.

9. Avoid giving clues in the question or statement stem.

10. Include clear directions for each item and each section of the assessment.

11. Leave time to prepare and to demonstrate performances.

12. Prepare enough materials and resources for learners to demonstrate performance expectations proficiently.

13. Be specific in the number of steps or activities the demonstrated performance should include.

14. Stipulate how the demonstrated performance will be scored.

15. Plan tasks that seek explanations and examples; avoid tasks that require demonstration of memorized information.

Table 8.7 Demonstrated Performance Suggestions for the Five Types of Inquiry and Information

Type of Inquiry and Information	Demonstrated Performance Prompts	Demonstrated Performance Suggestions
1. Recognition and recall	Who, What, Where, and When	• *Who:* Bring a photograph from home of the people who live with you. • *What:* Show what you can make with these three items. • *Where:* Open the book to the place where you can find a clue. • *When:* Find the time on the bus schedule when we will be returning.
2. Logic and reasoning	Why, Why not, and Explain	• *Why:* Show us why it is important to cover our mouths when we sneeze. • *Why not:* Create a collage displaying why we should not forget to recycle. • *Explain:* As a class, show me an explanation for the way Earth rotates.
3. Skills and applications	How, Point to, and Show me the steps	• *How:* Group the spheres to show the size and distance of the planets. • *Point to:* Point to the location on the map. • *Show me the steps:* Arrange the word cards to show me the steps of the science experiment.
4. Productivity and creativity	How else, What other way, and What else might happen	• *How else:* Move the pieces to show how else we can complete the puzzle. • *What other way:* Place the items differently to illustrate another way to plant the garden. • *What else might happen:* Show us what else we might do if we happen to have a fire drill.
5. Outlooks and dispositions	How do you feel, How does someone feel, and How might you feel if	• *How do you feel:* Model how you feel when someone unexpectedly does something nice for you. • *How does someone feel:* Show how someone feels when he or she makes a mistake in front of their friends. • *How might you feel if:* Show how you might feel if you are given the classroom Good Citizen Award.

process, diagnose possible learning difficulties, and provide immediate intervention as a correction or redirection. Demonstrated performances frequently offer the best or perhaps the only appraisal you can use to be sure the learner has gained proficiency.

As the student performs various activities to satisfy an inquiry or demonstrates understanding of information, other students can acquire new information too by watching and listening. When appraising with demonstrated performances, it is essential that expectations are established from the beginning and address content, process, and context. For example, if the learner is asked to model the correct revisions to a paragraph, the teacher should specify the expected changes matching the academic standards (content), the procedures involving the requested tools and equipment (processes), and the situation regarding available assistance, time limitations, and so forth (context). Demonstrated performances are a welcomed modification in the school day from the more frequently used appraisals of selected answers and written responses.

There are several disadvantages associated with demonstrated performances. They are time and energy consuming. For you to watch every learner show you a new skill requires that you move around the classroom quickly. This appraisal then becomes a classroom management challenge. How can you maintain order while learners are waiting for you to watch them perform a skill or task? You will have to decide if you will observe skills one at a time and privately or if you can watch many students performing the same skill at the same time, for example, math problems at the board. Either way, for you to provide intervention will take time away from the entire class.

Express Spoken Communications

Spoken communications are exchanged verbally through both formal and informal conversations and discussions that range from quite brief, such as one word, to longer explanations and presentations, such as book reports. Table 8.8 provides guidelines for constructing spoken communication assessment items.

Table 8.9 offers various instructions for the spoken communication form of appraisal for each of the five types of inquiry and information.

The advantages of spoken communications are everywhere. The classroom is a highly verbal environment. You talk with your learners and ask them unlimited numbers of questions every day, from greeting them first thing in the morning to probing their reasoning for understanding and applying new concepts. Inquiries and information

Table 8.8 Constructing Spoken Communications Assessment Items

1. Keep items short so they are spoken briefly.

2. Each item should assess only one expectation; don't overcomplicate the assessment.

3. Items should be communicated clearly and without ambiguity, with one correct response.

4. Distribute items for various kinds of spoken responses logically with other forms of appraisals.

5. Select a limited number of items for short answer and lengthier narratives; closely monitor the total time needed to complete the assessment.

6. Place items in a logical order.

7. Construct items that ask all five types of inquiry and information.

8. Use developmentally appropriate vocabulary and reading levels.

9. Avoid giving clues in the question or statement stem.

10. Include clear directions for each item and each section of the assessment.

11. Leave time to prepare the response perhaps using pencils and papers to prepare a response.

12. For shorter answers: Ask for only one example in the response.

13. For lengthier responses: Ask for a specific number of examples.

14. For all spoken responses: Stipulate how the content and oral mechanisms will be scored.

15. For all spoken responses: Ask questions that seek explanations and examples; avoid oral responses that require recitation of memorized information.

Table 8.9 Spoken Communications Suggestions for the Five Types of Inquiry and Information

Type of Inquiry and Information	Spoken Communications Prompts	Spoken Communications Suggestions
1. Recognition and recall	Who, What, Where, and When	• *Who:* Tell us who won the race. • *What:* Read what happened to the dog. • *Where:* Pronounce the location of the story. • *When:* Share with your group the date of the event.

(Continued)

Table 8.9 (Continued)

Type of Inquiry and Information	Spoken Communications Prompts	Spoken Communications Suggestions
2. Logic and reasoning	Why, Why not, and Explain	• *Why:* Give a reason why the girl was lost. • *Why not:* Tell your group why this is not the solution to the problem. • *Explain:* Describe an explanation to the situation.
3. Skills and applications	How, Point to, and Show me the steps	• *How:* Say aloud the steps for completing the math problem. • *Point to:* Define the words in each box. • *Show me the steps:* What is the name of this step of the process?
4. Productivity and creativity	How else, What other way, and What else might happen	• *How else:* Tell us how else you could take care of that situation. • *What other way:* Share with your partner another way to travel across the land. • *What else might happen:* What else might happen if we have an ice storm?
5. Outlooks and dispositions	How do you feel, How does someone feel, and How might you feel if	• *How do you feel:* Describe how you feel when there is a sudden change in our plans or the schedule. • *How does someone feel:* Tell us how you feel the main character felt with the change in plans. • *How might you feel if:* Share what you would feel if another student does not understand what you are trying to explain.

fluctuate among the many levels and ways of thinking. Through spoken communications, you can communicate quickly with your students and garner immediate feedback to reinforce or reroute your plans. Most teachers could not survive without appraising via spoken communications.

The disadvantages address the complexities that are associated with spoken communications. You can talk to the whole class, yet it is most effective for you to listen only to one learner at a time. Your intent of using spoken communications may be to appraise the cognitive domain, yet psychosocial and affective domains tend to enter spoken communications quickly, making your appraisals less clear.

Integrate Combined Forms of Appraisal

Combined forms of appraisal do just that: they combine picking selected answers with writing written responses (or perhaps with spoken communications) with demonstrated performances. For example, when your tenth grade students are learning math vocabulary, you show functions to the class and ask your students to repeat each new vocabulary word after you *say* the word aloud (spoken communications); you call on individual students to *point* to the specific function among a mixed group of functions (selected answers), and you ask the rest of the class to *say* aloud whether or not the pointing students were correct (spoken communications); you ask other learners to draw arrows from the vocabulary to *show* a function (demonstrated performances) and again you seek oral feedback from the class (spoken communications), then you ask each student to *write* the math vocabulary illustrated with the function on a sheet of paper (written responses). This example is a typical learning experience that happens in every middle-level and secondary school classroom multiple times each day. All forms of appraisal are in use, either in isolation or in combination.

Table 8.10 presents suggestions for constructing combined forms of appraisal assessment items; Table 8.11 shares suggested instructions

Table 8.10 Constructing Combined Forms of Appraisal Assessment Items

1. Keep items short by writing them on one line as often as possible or speaking them briefly.

2. Each item should assess only one expectation; don't overcomplicate the assessment.

3. Items should be written and/or spoken clearly clearly and without ambiguity, with one correct response.

4. Distribute items for various kinds of written or spoken responses logically with other forms of appraisals.

5. Select a limited number of items for short answer and written responses; closely monitor the total time needed to complete the assessment.

6. Place items in a logical order.

7. Include items that ask all five types of inquiry and information.

(Continued)

Table 8.10 (Continued)

8. Use developmentally appropriate vocabulary and reading levels.

9. Avoid giving clues in the question or statement stem.

10. Include clear directions for each item and each section of the assessment.

11. Leave time and space to write the response on the same side of the paper with the question.

12. For shorter answers: Ask for only one example in the response.

13. For lengthier responses: Ask for the specific number of examples.

14. For both written and spoken responses: Stipulate how the written and/or spoken content and writing mechanisms will be scored.

15. For both written and spoken responses: Ask questions that seek explanations and examples; avoid responses that require recitation of memorized information.

for the combined form of appraisal for each of the five types of inquiry and information.

The advantages of combined forms of appraisal are endless. When appraisals are combined, the assessments are more holistic, natural, and authentic. You are checking the learning, teaching, and schooling as they occur.

However, the major disadvantage of combined forms of appraisal is your need to isolate specific forms of appraisal. When you are interacting holistically and detect a concern, then you must concentrate on a particular form of appraisal to glean the necessary information. You will have to employ all forms of appraisal and think fast to cover your content, maintain classroom management, and still assess your learners.

Implement Assessments Purposefully

Each of the five forms of appraisal offers an assortment of choices that address different purposes. They present seemingly endless opportunities to be creative, enhance the learning and teaching, and involve your learners so they have voice, choice, and agency in the classroom. Assessments can be direct, integrated, or embedded. *Direct assessments* are connected explicitly between the task and the

Table 8.11   Combined Forms of Appraisal Suggestions for the Five Types
of Inquiry and Information

Type of Inquiry and Information	Prompts	Combined Forms of Appraisal Suggestions
1. Recognition and recall	Who, What, Where, and When	• *Who:* Tell me the main character in the story and read a paragraph that describes the character. • *What:* Answer the math problem and arrange the manipulatives to show the answer. • *Where:* Draw a political cartoon of your idea and write a caption for your cartoon. • *When:* Move the hands on the clock to the time in three time zones.
2. Logic and reasoning	Why, Why not, and Explain	• *Why:* With a partner, write one way to demonstrate citizenship on a card but do not show it to the class; then show this way to the class for everyone to guess what is written on your card. • *Why not:* Tell the members of your group one reason why the solution to the math problem is not correct; then solve the problem correctly as a group. • *Explain:* Write the steps to the science experiment and share them with the class.
3. Skills and applications	How, Point to, and Show me the steps	• *How:* Select the three stages of the geographic changes and place them in the correct order. • *Point to:* Point to the paragraph in the book that tells about the president and recap the information in your own words. • *Show me the steps:* Label the steps for solving the math problem on the board; select one step and explain its importance.
4. Productivity and creativity	How else, What other way, and What else might happen	• *How else:* Explain another way the character knew what was happening and add your idea to the list on the board. • *What other way:* Show the class another way to organize the materials and describe the steps as you go. • *What else might happen:* Write an ending to the story telling what else might happen; then draw a picture and show it to your partner while you read your new ending aloud.

(Continued)

Table 8.11 (Continued)

Type of Inquiry and Information	Prompts	Combined Forms of Appraisal Suggestions
5. Outlooks and dispositions	*How do you feel, How does someone feel, and How might you feel if*	• *How do you feel:* Show and tell how you feel when you eat something that is new and you discover that you like it. • *How does someone feel:* Write five words telling how someone feels when he or she is frightened at school; then show how to overcome the fear. • *How might you feel if:* From the pictures on the board, pick one and write two paragraphs describing the picture. Do not share your paragraphs. When asked, read your paragraphs aloud for other students to guess your picture. Then display your paragraphs next to the picture.

*11 possibilities: *Pick and write; Pick and show; Pick and say; Write and show; Write and say; Say and show; Pick, write, and show; Pick, write, and say; Pick, show, and say; Write, show, and say; Pick, write, show, and say.*

desired outcome; for example, calculating the sums for 10 addition problems. *Integrated assessments* blend the expectations for one academic subject area together with the expectations for another academic subject area; for example, reading and solving 10 math problems. *Embedded assessments* include several expectations that are intricately involved in one overall assessment; for example, determining the amount of new carpet to order for a room. The student must measure, calculate, read carpet specifications, and so forth. Although the student is completing one task, many different appraisals are embedded in the task.

As you develop your performance-based assessment, you want to fulfill these three overarching guidelines.

1. Consistently use all five forms of appraisal so you broaden the teaching and gather evidence of progress from every way your learners can express themselves.

2. Selectively balance using a variety of forms of appraisal so you establish a comfortable routine yet avoid a predictable rut.

3. Meticulously plan your forms of appraisal and maintain records of your assessments so you know the times and frequency that you have used your selected forms.

Include Various Appraisal Tasks

The five types of appraisals allow you to align the assessments with your curriculum and instruction to highlight a variety of tasks. You can use any of the five forms of appraisal as direct, integrated, or embedded appraisals to assess:

- Analysis perspectives tasks
- Application tasks
- Classifications tasks
- Comparison tasks
- Decision-making tasks
- Error identification tasks
- Experimental tasks
- Historical perspectives tasks
- Inventions tasks
- Position support tasks
- Predictions tasks
- Problem-solving tasks

Clarify Directions

You must clarify your directions for every form of appraisal. If you are writing your directions, practice saying them aloud to yourself and listen closely. Pretend you are one of your own learners. Or ask one of your trusted colleagues to complete the assessment and give you feedback so you can clarify the directions.

Here are some questions to ask yourself: *Do the directions make sense? Do you need to include an example in the directions? Are you seeking only one task at a time? Have you included directions for each section of the assessment, especially if different sections conduct different forms of appraisal? Do you have enough space on the paper to complete each item and task on the assessment? Have you provided the necessary tools and/or technology to complete each item and task appropriately? Have you allowed enough time to complete the entire assessment?* You might be surprised to find you have constructed the assessment for a well-informed adult rather than for one of your own students.

You also want to be sure that your learners have practiced the types of assessments with the same or similar directions prior to the actual assessment. After all, your intent is to assess your learners' knowledge and skills; you are not trying to assess their abilities to comprehend your directions.

If you are giving oral directions, prepare them well in advance by writing them on a piece of paper or on note cards. Oral directions require that you cover the content, assess each learner as thoroughly as you can, provide feedback with appropriate interventions, and keep records on everyone's progress. You will not be able to remember how well each learner participated in oral assessments, so you must have prepared a copy of the class roster with space where you can note anecdotal records.

Seek Balance

It is usual for classroom teachers to use the same forms of appraisals repeatedly in various subject areas. You want to become keenly aware of your patterns by keeping accurate records. You can record your form of appraisal in your daily lesson plans or calendar. Most likely, you will discover that you have established a routine that could use some expansion and variation. No doubt, your learners are more attuned to your patterns than you are.

Try using a different form of appraisal every day; mix up your forms of appraisal so you are using all forms in all subject areas and are not relegating specific forms of appraisals to specific subject areas. Some teachers are not even aware of their own routines; however, your students *will* be attuned and prepared for your routines. Now is your chance to be creative and help your students grow. For example, if you use pencil-and-paper assessments primarily with selected answers, try using more written responses or combined forms by adding demonstrated performances. Remember that learners remember the greatest amounts of information by teaching one another. Let them teach one another as often as possible.

Give Learners Choices

Try to give your learners choices in the forms of appraisals, too. As the school year progresses and you have used all five forms of appraisal, tell your learners that for the next book report, they have choices. You design samples in some or all forms of appraisal from which they can choose. Learners can sign a "contract" letting you know they understand the expectation. You and your whole class will learn much more when your students express their outcomes in a variety of ways.

Once your learners become accustomed to having choices in the forms of appraisal, you and they can collaboratively develop the choices of performance-based assessments. This is your ultimate quest. Now you have equipped your students to plan and organize their own learning. Congratulations!

Develop Appraisals to Showcase Learning . . .

Your appraisals should offer opportunities for your learners to highlight their accomplishments. Sadly, too many teachers use appraisals to prove to their students or the students' families what their students don't know or can't do. If your learners are not assessing well, you need to revisit your teaching and the schooling. Appraisals serve as the capstone of curriculum, instruction, and assessment that are all aligned and synchronized for success.

Extend With Questions and Activities

Frequently Asked Questions

1. **What can I do to balance my formative assessments with my summative assessments?**

As you plan your curriculum and instruction for the upcoming units of learning, start brainstorming ideas that use each of the five forms of appraisal. Incorporate the five forms throughout the unit as formative assessments; then pull a few examples of each formative assessment into the summative assessment at the end of the unit.

2. **How can I be sure than I am using all five forms of appraisal with all learners?**

This is an important challenge for you to realize. You will know which learners prefer to pick, write, say, show, or respond using combined forms. You need to build upon strengths yet improve weaknesses.

3. **How do I involve my learners' families in my assessments?**

Communicate with your learners' families at the start of the school year through a newsletter and Web site. Give them an example of all five fives of appraisal and reasons for using all five forms. At parent-teacher conferences, you can discuss the five forms with the families and find out which forms they think are best for their children.

Activities

1. Select one subject area, such as spelling. What are examples of the five forms of appraisal that you can use to assess your learners' spelling progress?

2. Reflect on your own assignments, projects, tests, and so forth. What was your favorite form of appraisal? Did you prefer selecting an answer, writing a response, showing your knowledge, telling the outcomes, or combining two or more forms of appraisal? Why did you prefer this form of appraisal, and, how do you think your past patterns will influence your teaching practices?

3. Make a copy of the chart showing the five forms of appraisal and authentication Keep a record of the five types of assessment that you, a colleague, or your cooperative classroom mentor teacher uses. What does this data tell you?

4. Practice writing a form of appraisal that is new or different for you. Why have you been avoiding using this form of appraisal for this subject area? What are the benefits for you and your learners of using a different form of appraisal in this particular subject area?

5. Identify the favorite form of appraisal for each student and develop a different one for the students to use during a future unit of learning. Compare and contrast your learners' levels of achievement.

9

Creating Assessment Templates and Rubrics

There are two important tools to help you plan, organize, and monitor the learning and teaching. The first one is called a *template,* a graphic organizer that unites the five types of information and the five forms of appraisal into a convenient and practical tool for you to develop 25 assessments related to a single theme or topic. You can copy the template and use it with every learning experience and unit of learning. By keeping your templates on file on your computer and with your written plans, you can keep track of the various kinds of performance-based assessments you use for gathering baseline data, formative data, and summative data throughout the school year.

Then you can monitor how you assess the learning and the learners, the teaching and the teacher, and the curriculum and content. Performance-based assessments provide insightful feedback in all three areas that you want to evaluate continuously. To be an effective teacher, your accountability includes all three areas, and the template will allow you to gather the data quickly and easily.

The second tool is the *rubric,* another graphic organizer to help you and your learners plan, organize, and monitor progress. A rubric is a tool to identify outcomes, determine values for each outcome, and record achievement for each outcome. You can create on your own in advance of the learning and teaching, or you can create collaboratively with your learners. Several extremely important characteristics define rubrics and the kinds of rubrics you can and want to use in your classroom. Guidelines delineating effective rubrics are presented later in this chapter.

Construct the Assessment Template

Table 9.1, the assessment template, has been divided into two sections that fit across the pages of this book. You can make a copy to fit on one sheet of paper by setting your computer in landscape mode. The assessment template can be completed readily on one sheet of paper and stored easily in a notebook for quick reference.

Notice that the five forms of appraisal and authentication are listed in a row across the top of the template and the five types of inquiry information are listed in a column on the left. You can complete the template by starting with the forms of appraisal or the types of information. And you can begin in any cell that first grabs your interest. This way you can use various kinds of performance-based assessments that are your and your learners' favorites while ensuring that you use many different kinds of assessments.

Additionally, you can move any of your performance-based assessments around as you plan and align your curriculum and instruction for a specific unit of learning. By keeping records of all your units of learning, you can monitor the performance-based assessments that you have used, that have been effective, and that you need to use more often to help your learners stretch and grow.

Complete a Sample Template

Let's start with the cells under the form of appraisal labeled "Selected Answers." Next look at the five types of inquiry and information. Write a sample assessment item in the cell. For example, for a ninth grade literacy unit of learning on writing a five-sentence paragraph, you could fill the cell "Recognition and recall" with: "Place an X next to the complete paragraphs." Remember, all "Selected Answers" require the learner to *pick* an answer. This assessment could be conducted as a preassessment to gather baseline data; the assessment would include ten samples, some of which are complete paragraphs and some of which are not complete paragraphs.

Now let's fill the four other cells under "Selected Answers." Next to "Logic and reasoning," a sample assessment might read: "Fill in the dot to the left of the sentence that is the best sentence to finish the paragraph." Next to "Skills and applications," a sample assessment might read: "Match the incorrect section of each paragraph to the correct section of the paragraph." Next to "Productivity and creativity," a sample assessment might read: "Draw a line from each missing label of the paragraph parts to the correct label." Next to "Outlooks and dispositions," a sample assessment might read: "Mark A, B, C, or D for the message the paragraph is communicating." (See Table 9.2 for a template completed with these examples.)

Let's start another assessment template. For a sixth grade math unit of learning on finding perimeter and area, you could fill the cell under the form of appraisal headed "Written Responses" for the type of information labeled "Logic and reasoning" with: "Write a short reason telling why the sum to each problem is correct or not correct." This assessment could be conducted as an in class assignment completed in small groups of three learners to gather formative data; the assessment would include 20 problems with 10 correct calculations and 10 incorrect calculations. More assessment items are included in the template. More assessment items are included in the example template presented in Table 9.3.

Here's the start of an example for "Demonstrated Performances." For a seventh grade science unit on the water cycle, you could fill the cell under the form of appraisal headed "Demonstrated Performances" for the type of information labeled "Skills and applications" with: "Point to where condensation occurs," "Point to where evaporation occurs," and so forth. This assessment would be conducted individually to gather summative data; the assessment would include asking learners to draw and explain the water cycle in various U.S. geographic locations. More assessment items are included in the example template presented in Table 9.4.

Next, Table 9.5 presents the start for a template for "Spoken Communications" for an integrated twelfth grade science and social studies unit on environment. More assessment items are included in the template cells.

Finally, you can combine all forms of appraisal. These are your opportunities to make the learning holistic, natural, and authentic.

It is vital that you recognize the many roles of performance-based assessments. Although this example gathers summative data, effective teachers realize that most summative data also serves as formative data or baseline data. If you are the seventh grade teacher administering this assessment on the water cycle, and you realize that any of your learners is challenged by this assessment, you must

(Text continues on page 182)

Table 9.1 Template of Performance-Based Assessments

	Five Forms of Appraisal and Authentication	
Types of Inquiry and Information	*Selected Answers* Prompt: *Pick*	*Written Responses* Prompt: *Write* ⟶
1. Recognition and recall *Who, What, Where,* and *When*		
2. Logic and reasoning *Why, Why not,* and *Explain*		
3. Skills and applications *How, Point to,* and *Show me the steps*		
4. Productivity and creativity *How else, What other way,* and *What else might happen*		
5. Outlooks and dispositions *How do you feel, How does someone feel,* and *How might you feel if*		

Demonstrated Performances Prompt: *Show*	Spoken Communications Prompt: *Say*	Combined Forms Prompts: *11 possibilities**

*11 possibilities: *Pick and write; Pick and show; Pick and say; Write and show; Write and say; Say and show; Pick, write, and show; Pick, write, and say; Pick, show, and say; Write, show, and say; Pick, write, show, and say.*

Table 9.2 Ninth Grade Literacy Unit: Five-Sentence Paragraph, Selected Answers Only

Types of Inquiry and Information	Selected Answers Prompt: *Pick*	Five Forms of Appraisal and Authentication			
		Written Responses Prompt: *Write*	Demonstrated Performances Prompt: *Show*	Spoken Communications Prompt: *Say*	Combined Forms Prompts: *11 possibilities**
1. Recognition and recall *Who, What, Where,* and *When*	Place an X next to the complete paragraphs.				
2. Logic and reasoning *Why, Why not,* and *Explain*	Fill in the dot to the left of the sentence that is the best sentence to finish the paragraph.				
3. Skills and applications *How, Point to,* and *Show me the steps*	Match the incorrect section of each paragraph to the correct section of the paragraph.				
4. Productivity and creativity *How else, What other way,* and *What else might happen*	Draw a line from each missing label of the paragraph parts to the correct label.				
5. Outlooks and dispositions *How do you feel, How does someone feel,* and *How might you feel if*	Mark A, B, C, or D for the message the paragraph is communicating.				

*11 possibilities: *Pick and write; Pick and show; Pick and say; Write and show; Write and say; Say and show; Pick, write, and show; Pick, write, and say; Pick, show, and say; Write, show, and say; Pick, write, show, and say.*

Table 9.3 Sixth Grade Math: Calculating Perimeter, Area, and Volume

Types of Inquiry and Information	Five Forms of Appraisal and Authentication				
	Selected Answers Prompt: Pick	Written Responses Prompt: Write	Demonstrated Performances Prompt: Show	Spoken Communications Prompt: Say	Combined Forms Prompts: 11 possibilities*
1. Recognition and recall *Who, What, Where,* and *When*		Solve the problems by calculating the perimeter, area, or volume.			
2. Logic and reasoning *Why, Why not,* and *Explain*		Write a short reason telling why the calculation to each problem is either correct or not correct.			
3. Skills and applications *How, Point to,* and *Show me the steps*		Construct a five-sentence paragraph explaining how to calculate perimeter, area, and volume.			
4. Productivity and creativity *How else, What other way,* and *What else might happen*		Design one word problem each to calculate the perimeter, area, and volume.			
5. Outlooks and dispositions *How do you feel, How does someone feel,* and *How might you feel if*		Create your reason for learning how to calculate perimeter, area, and volume.			

*11 possibilities: *Pick and write; Pick and show; Pick and say; Write and show; Write and say; Say and show; Pick, write, and show; Pick, write, and say; Pick, show, and say; Write, show, and say; Pick, write, show, and say.*

Table 9.4 Seventh Grade Science: Water Cycle, Demonstrated Performances Only

Types of Inquiry and Information	Five Forms of Appraisal and Authentication				
	Selected Answers Prompt: Pick	Written Responses Prompt: Write	Demonstrated Performances Prompt: Show	Spoken Communications Prompt: Say	Combined Forms Prompts: 11 possibilities*
1. Recognition and recall *Who, What, Where, and When*			Select one of the vocabulary word cards related to the water cycle and ask someone in the class to spell the word and describe its function.		
2. Logic and reasoning *Why, Why not, and Explain*			Draw the water cycle on a large poster allowing space for identification and explanation.		
3. Skills and applications *How, Point to, and Show me the steps*			Show how the water cycle functions in various U.S. geographic		
4. Productivity and creativity *How else, What other way, and What else might happen*			Demonstrate how people feel in general during various times of the water cycle.		
5. Outlooks and dispositions *How do you feel, How does someone feel, and How might you feel if*			Take one of the vocabulary word cards related to the water cycle and ask someone in the class to spell the word and describe its function.		

*11 possibilities: *Pick and write; Pick and show; Pick and say; Write and show; Write and say; Say and show; Pick, write, and show; Pick, write, and say; Pick, show, and say; Write, show, and say; Pick, write, show, and say.*

Table 9.5 Twelfth Grade Science and Social Studies: The Environment, Spoken Communications Only

Types of Inquiry and Information	Five Forms of Appraisal and Authentication				
	Selected Answers Prompt: *Pick*	Written Responses Prompt: *Write*	Demonstrated Performances Prompt: *Show*	Spoken Communications Prompt: *Say*	Combined Forms Prompts: 11 possibilities*
1. Recognition and recall *Who, What, Where, and When*				Tell what is meant by the term *environment*.	
2. Logic and reasoning *Why, Why not, and Explain*				Explain why the environment is both a science topic and a political issue.	
3. Skills and applications *How, Point to, and Show me the steps*				Describe how people interact with the environment.	
4. Productivity and creativity *How else, What other way, and What else might happen*				Share one creative idea for making your environment healthier and safer.	
5. Outlooks and dispositions *How do you feel, How does someone feel, and How might you feel if*				Give one suggestion that you wish more people knew about taking care of the environment.	

*11 possibilities: Pick and write; Pick and show; Pick and say; Write and show; Write and say; Say and show; Pick, write, and show; Pick, write, and say; Pick, show, and say; Write, show, and say; Pick, write, show, and say.

revisit and reteach the student learning expectations. You will decide the best approaches for reteaching and assessing the expectation. Most likely, you will administer another set of performance-based assessments to gather both formative and summative data.

Remember: All interactions and assignments are performance-based assessments, and the most effective assessments generate feedback and formative data that guide you and your learners. The overarching task is to consider the six components of assessment: your learners and their learning, you and your teaching, and the school and schooling (see Chapter 1) all at once as you identify one form of appraisal for each type of information. *How* do you want your learners to provide you evidence of *what* they know, do, and believe?

Examine Template Examples

Following are four completed template examples based on student learning expectations taken from a variety of state standards. You are urged to mix, match, modify, and develop your own assessments to fit the learning, teaching, and schooling in your environment and sociocultural context. Table 9.6 introduces a sixth grade integrated language arts and social studies unit of learning on transportation. Table 9.7 presents a tenth grade science unit of learning on plants. Table 9.8 describes an eighth grade math unit of learning on geometric shapes. Table 9.9 details an eleventh grade literacy unit of learning on conflict.

Build Rubrics

Rubrics are rating scales that identify and list the criteria that the learner must know, do, and believe to achieve the desired outcomes. Thus, rubrics are criterion referenced. Most rubrics stipulate the level of quality that the learner must demonstrate in order to earn a particular score or grade. At least three levels are identified, with groups of characteristics to accompany each level. The groups of characteristics and criteria or items that make up a level are called *benchmarks*. It is essential that rubrics are given to students early during the learning and teaching. Rubrics serve as the schedule, agenda, and frame for the unit of learning.

Rubrics tend to be presented as a graphic organizer, designed as a grid with the criteria listed vertically in the column on the left of the grid and the levels or benchmarks listed horizontally in a row across the top of the grid, as shown in Table 9.10. Some rubrics are called *holistic rubrics,* as shown in Table 9.11; they cluster all of the criteria in one box or cell so the product is rated one time as being closest that criteria. Some rubrics are called *analytic rubrics,* as shown in Table 9.12; they separate the criteria and list each item individually, so criteria are rated individually. A final assessment is determined from the individual ratings.

The ratings may be recorded as numbers or checkmarks in columns that correspond to numbers or grades. Table 9.11 shows a holistic rubric with 10 criteria for each of three anticipated levels. Criteria relating to both the content and the mechanics of this writing assignments are included in each level. This rubric will be distributed when learners are given the assignment to write a paragraph describing an event.

If the learner exceeds the assignment expectations, the learner has demonstrated the qualities of the column on the left. If the learner completes the assignment expectations satisfactorily, then the learner has demonstrated the qualities of the column in the middle. If the learner does not complete the assignment expectations satisfactorily, then the learner has demonstrated the qualities of the column on the right. In the analytic rubric, shown in Table 9.12, the three levels of 10 criteria or qualities for writing a paragraph are divided by the number of points the student can earn for each criterion. In the holistic rubric, points are given for the entire assignment. When a student achieves the criteria for the level or benchmark of Proficient, the student fulfills the benchmark and earns a score of 3. When a student achieves the criteria for the level of Satisfactory, the student fulfills this benchmark and earns a score of 2. Likewise, when a student does not achieve the level of Satisfactory, the student falls into the benchmark of Unsatisfactory and earns a score of 1.

Some rubrics are designed so that the levels read horizontally across the top row from low to high or high to low. You can place the levels on your rubrics in either direction. The consensus stemming from conversations with teachers, learners at all ages and stages, as well as many parents of young learners, reveals that most people advocate labeling the levels high to low as you read left to right. Individuals who either read or score the rubric report that they like to focus on the first column and set their sights on the highest level of achievement. My own students and I have found it most convenient to stop at the first column, so that should be the highest level of achievement.

(Text continues on page 192)

Table 9.6   Sixth Grade Integrated Language Arts and Social Studies: Transportation

Types of Inquiry and Information	Five Forms of Appraisal and Authentication	
	Selected Answers Prompt: *Pick*	Written Responses Prompt: *Write*
1. Recognition and recall *Who, What, Where,* and *When*	Match each sentence on the left describing a mode of transportation with the one correct diagram on the right by drawing a line between them.	Fill in the blank with a word that makes the sentence about modes of transportation make sense.
2. Logic and reasoning *Why, Why not,* and *Explain*	Circle T for True or F for False next to each phrase explaining why each mode of transportation is the best one in the situation.	Write one sentence using the transportation word.
3. Skills and applications *How, Point to,* and *Show me the steps*	Place an X to the left of the correct word to complete each sentence describing the uses for these modes of transportation.	Give two ways people use this item as a mode of transportation.
4. Productivity and creativity *How else, What other way,* and *What else might happen*	Select the best answer and underline it describing a change over time for each mode of transportation.	Describe a newly invented mode of transportation.
5. Outlooks and dispositions *How do you feel, How does someone feel,* and *How might you feel if*	Check each item in the list that describes how you feel when you ride your bicycle.	Construct a sentence about how people feel about each mode of transportation.

Demonstrated Performances Prompt: *Show*	Spoken Communications Prompt: *Say*	Combined Forms Prompts: *11 possibilities**
Show us how people use the mode of transportation shown on the card.	Read aloud the name of the transportation on your list.	Select a category and tell us three examples of this mode of transportation that fit into the category.
Demonstrate three ways that people use a mode of transportation in different situations.	Explain why this particular item is and is not a mode of transportation.	Write one sentence that describes a mode of transportation but leave out the word. Then ask your partner to fill in the blank.
Draw a picture of how a mode of transportation is a tool that helps us.	Describe aloud a mode of transportation used only for entertainment.	Tell us about a mode of transportation that was more important in the past.
Create a picture of your invented mode of transportation.	Tell us a story about an adventure on any mode of transportation.	Design a picture of transportation unique to a country other than the United States.
Show us how people feel when traveling on the mode of transportation on the word card.	Justify why people like to travel.	Predict the first automobile you'll want to have when you are an adult.

*11 possibilities: *Pick and write; Pick and show; Pick and say; Write and show; Write and say; Say and show; Pick, write, and show; Pick, write, and say; Pick, show, and say; Write, show, and say; Pick, write, show, and say.*

Table 9.7   Tenth Grade Science: Plants

| Types of Inquiry and Information | Five Forms of Appraisal and Authentication | |
	Selected Answers Prompt: *Pick*	Written Responses Prompt: *Write*
1. Recognition and recall *Who, What, Where,* and *When*	Draw a line to connect the word on the left with the plant on the right.	Fill in the blank with the name of the plant.
2. Logic and reasoning *Why, Why not,* and *Explain*	Circle T for true and F for False for each sentence that applies to the plants of the identified region.	Explain two examples of plants in our region in writing.
3. Skills and applications *How, Point to,* and *Show me the steps*	Fill in the blank with a word from the list to name the plant.	Write a sentence to describe a plant.
4. Productivity and creativity *How else, What other way,* and *What else might happen*	Select the plant that fits with the category of plants.	Create a new plant and describe it in three paragraphs.
5. Outlooks and dispositions *How do you feel, How does someone feel,* and *How might you feel if*	Pick the best answer that completes each sentence about plants in various contexts.	Construct a paragraph to convey feelings associated with plants.

Demonstrated Performances Prompt: *Show*	Spoken Communications Prompt: *Say*	Combined Forms Prompts: *11 possibilities**
Show the commonly found plants in our region.	Describe the name of the plant on the card.	Select a word card and draw the plant.
Group the word cards together with the correct plant category.	Read aloud the description of the plant.	Make a list of all the plants you see in these pictures and share your list with your group members.
Place the names of the parts of the plants on the drawing.	Tell us where you see this plant when you look at the picture.	Draw a picture of plants that could be added to the school grounds.
Use the manipulatives to create a new and funky plant.	As the group describes a plant, call out its name.	Design a picture of a new plant; give it a name, and write three sentences about it.
Show us how a plant makes you feel.	Justify why a plant makes you feel the way it does.	Write and conduct a survey of the class about their favorite plants for different times and situations.

*11 possibilities: *Pick and write; Pick and show; Pick and say; Write and show; Write and say; Say and show; Pick, write, and show; Pick, write, and say; Pick, show, and say; Write, show, and say; Pick, write, show, and say.*

Table 9.8   Eighth Grade Math: Geometric Shapes

	Five Forms of Appraisal and Authentication	
Types of Inquiry and Information	*Selected Answers* Prompt: *Pick*	*Written Responses* Prompt: *Write*
1. Recognition and recall *Who, What, Where,* and *When*	Draw a line to connect the word on the left with the shape on the right.	Fill in the blank with the name of the shape.
2. Logic and reasoning *Why, Why not,* and *Explain*	Circle T for true and F for False for each sentence that applies to the shapes.	Identify two examples of circles in our classroom in writing.
3. Skills and applications *How, Point to,* and *Show me the steps*	Fill in the blank with a word from the list to name the shape.	Write a word problem using geometric shapes.
4. Productivity and creativity *How else, What other way,* and *What else might happen*	Select the shape that fits with the category of shapes.	Using five different shapes create a new shape and describe it in writing.
5. Outlooks and dispositions *How do you feel, How does someone feel,* and *How might you feel if*	Pick the best answer that completes each sentence about shapes in our everyday lives.	Construct a sentence and include shapes to convey feelings.

Demonstrated Performances Prompt: *Show*	Spoken Communications Prompt: *Say*	Combined Forms Prompts: *11 possibilities**
Show me the shape of a common found item.	Tell me the name of the shape on the card.	Select a word card and draw the shape.
Group the word cards together with the correct shape.	Read aloud the description of the shape.	Make a list of all the squares you see in our classroom and share your list with your group members.
Place each math manipulative together to form the shape stated on the word card.	Explain where you see this shape when we write letters and words.	Draw a picture using shapes to make a piece of playground equipment.
Use the math manipulatives to create a new and funky shape.	As the group makes a shape, call out its name.	Design a picture of a new shape, give it a name, and write three sentences about it.
Act how a shape makes you feel.	Describe why a shape makes you feel the way it does.	Write and conduct a survey of the class about their favorite shapes.

*11 possibilities: *Pick and write; Pick and show; Pick and say; Write and show; Write and say; Say and show; Pick, write, and show; Pick, write, and say; Pick, show, and say; Write, show, and say; Pick, write, show, and say.*

Table 9.9 Eleventh Grade Literacy: Conflict

Types of Inquiry and Information	Five Forms of Appraisal and Authentication	
	Selected Answers Prompt: *Pick*	Identify Responses Prompt: *Write*
1. Recognition and recall *Who, What, Where,* and *When*	Fill in the blank from the vocabulary list with the correct word about conflict.	Identify the type of conflict that makes each sentence correct.
2. Logic and reasoning *Why, Why not,* and *Explain*	Look at the picture and select the best answer that describes the conflict.	Write a sentence that differentiates different types of conflict.
3. Skills and applications *How, Point to,* and *Show me the steps*	Connect the description of the conflict with the correct name of the conflict.	Construct the directions for relieving conflict in each of the situations identified.
4. Productivity and creativity *How else, What other way,* and *What else might happen*	Mark each statement T for True or F for False next to each statement about conflict.	Create a short story in which conflict plays a major role.
5. Outlooks and dispositions *How do you feel, How does someone feel,* and *How might you feel if*	Underline the word that describes how the conflict in each situation makes people feel in general.	Pen a poem about conflict and people's outlooks.

Demonstrated Performances Prompt: *Show*	Spoken Communications Prompt: *Say*	*Combined Forms* Prompts: *11 possibilities**
Act like one type of conflict; your partner will guess what you are demonstrating.	Read aloud the list of words about conflict and their descriptors.	Select one of the vocabulary words about conflict and draw a picture for us to guess what you are showing.
Draw three models for coping with conflict.	Tell the class why it is important for us to be aware of conflict and what it does to and for us.	Listen to a passage read aloud by a member of the class and tell the class what it means.
Create two endings to a scene in which a person encounters a personal conflict.	Explain how conflict is a part of our everyday interactions and helps us grow.	Identify signs of conflict and how we can avoid conflict in a work setting.
With the members of your group, construct an exercise to help people cope with conflict.	Share a time that you overcame conflict positively and productively.	Draw three pictures of how people around the world prepare for different types of conflict.
Show us how people should react and should not react during a public conflict.	Describe how conflict can make people feel differently.	Make a list of how conflict and growth are the same and different.

*11 possibilities: *Pick and write; Pick and show; Pick and say; Write and show; Write and say; Say and show; Pick, write, and show; Pick, write, and say; Pick, show, and say; Write, show, and say; Pick, write, show, and say.*

Table 9.10   Rubric With Three Levels or Benchmarks

High: Proficient	Medium: Satisfactory	Low: Unsatisfactory

Table 9.11   Sample Rubric With Three Levels and 10 Criteria

High: Proficient	Medium: Satisfactory	Low: Unsatisfactory
A 30 points	B 20 points	C 10 points
• Student writes more than one paragraph	• Student writes one paragraph	• Student writes less than one paragraph
• All sentences are complete	• All sentences are complete	• Some sentences are not complete
• Description is creative	• Description is adequate	• Description is inadequate
• Vocabulary is advanced	• Vocabulary is basic	• Vocabulary is below basic
• Sequence of events captivates reader	• Sequence of events makes sense	• Sequence of events does not make sense
• Grammar, punctuation, and spelling are exemplary	• Grammar, punctuation, and spelling are adequate	• Grammar, punctuation, and spelling need attention
• Paragraph is exciting to read	• Paragraph is easy to understand	• Paragraph is not easy to understand
• Author writes completely independently	• Author writes independently or with little assistance	• Author needs much assistance
• Paper is completed on time or early	• Paper is completed on time	• Paper is late
• Paper is neat and easy to read	• Paper is neat	• Paper is not neat

It is highly recommended that you look at the rubrics used by your school and colleagues so you follow their pattern. Or, if you decide to design your own pattern of rubrics, be sure to communicate your design with your learners and their families prior to using them to score outcomes.

Table 9.12 Eighth Grade Analytic Writing Rubric

High: Proficient		Medium: Satisfactory		Low: Unsatisfactory	
3	*21–30 points*	2	*11–20 points*	1	*0–10 points*
Student writes more than one paragraph	3	Student writes one paragraph	2	Student writes less than one paragraph	1
All sentences are complete	3	All sentences are complete	2	Some sentences are not complete	1
Description is creative	3	Description is adequate	2	Description is inadequate	1
Vocabulary is advanced	3	Vocabulary is basic	2	Vocabulary is below basic	1
Sequence of events captivates reader	3	Sequence of events makes sense	2	Sequence of events does not make sense	1
Grammar, punctuation, and spelling are exemplary	3	Grammar, punctuation, and spelling need a little attention	2	Grammar, punctuation, and spelling need much attention	1
Paragraph is exciting to read	3	Paragraph is easy to understand	2	Paragraph is not easy to understand	1
Author writes completely independently	3	Author writes independently or with little assistance	2	Author needs much assistance	1
Paper is completed on time or early	3	Paper is completed on time	2	Paper is late	1
Paper is neat and easy to read	3	Paper is neat	2	Paper is not neat	1
Subtotal		Subtotal		Subtotal	
GRAND TOTAL					

Follow the 3 × 3 × 3 Model

Determining which criteria or expected items to cluster with each level is challenging, so it is recommended that you follow the 3 × 3 × 3 Model, at least to get started. You may discover that the 3 × 3 × 3 Model fits your needs and you will use it all the time.

The 3 × 3 × 3 Model means that there are at least:

- Three levels identified horizontally across the top row with the highest level starting on the left
- Three criteria identified vertically down the left column serving as starters or stems to three sorts of evidence. One criterion should relate to qualitative evidence. One criterion should relate to quantitative evidence. And one criterion should relate to connective evidence. Connective evidence allows the student to contextualize and demonstrate outcomes in ways that make personal meaning for the student.
- Three sorts of evidence within the cells that include qualitative knowledge, quantitative skills, and connections with dispositions related to the theme or topic of learning

Table 9.13 is blank copy of a 3 × 3 × 3 Model rubric.

You understand the three levels or benchmarks and the three criteria. Now let's examine the three sorts of evidence—knowledge, skills, and dispositions—or what you want your learners to know, do, and believe at the end of the unit of learning or individual learning experience. Let's say you are preparing a unit of learning about maps with seventh graders. You consult your school district and state student learning expectations that connect with the five types of inquiries and information (see Chapter 7). You create activities and assignments for your learners to read, write, produce, talk, and show their learning in all five forms of appraisal and authentication (see Chapter 8).

As you design the rubric for the unit for you to score their outcomes, you want to be sure that you have included knowledge, skills, and dispositions. For example, if your learners are going to create their own countries, the expectations could include preparing an encyclopedia like entries describing the physical geography, the cultural geography, and the social structures; drawing maps of the country with keys and legends; and writing the history and social interactions reflecting the industrial endeavors and recreational pastimes of the people. The unit expectations now include qualitative knowledge, quantitative skills, and connections with dispositions fulfilling the third portion of the 3 × 3 × 3 Model. Another example is shown in Table 9.14.

Table 9.13 3 × 3 × 3 Model Rubric

Criteria	Proficient	Satisfactory	Unsatisfactory
Qualitative			
Quantitative			
Connections			

Table 9.14   Sample 3 × 3 × 3 Rubric: Math Word Problem Converting
Fractions Into Decimals

Criteria	Proficient	Satisfactory	Unsatisfactory
Qualitative	Writes the word problem in a way that fulfills or exceeds the tasks, is clear and easy to follow, with no errors	Writes the word problem in a way that fulfills the task and is clear and easy to follow, with few errors	Does not write the word problem in a way that fulfills the task and is clear and easy to follow, or writes with many errors
Quantitative	Shows the calculation to prove that the word problem can be solved two different ways	Shows the calculation to prove that the word problem can be solved	Does not show the calculation or does not prove that the word problem can be solved
Connections	Places the word problem in a commonly found situation with which most people can identify	Places the word problem in a commonly found situation	Does not place the word problem in a commonly found situation

Use All Kinds of Rubrics

Rubrics can be used with individual activities and assignments for a particular learning experience or for an entire unit of learning. Creating a template is ideal for preparing your rubrics for an entire unit. There are eight primary kinds of rubrics: analytic rubrics, holistic rubrics, checklists, chronological, longitudinal, process, product, and rating scale rubrics.

1. *Analytic rubrics.* The analytic rubric describes the individual parts or specific items of the product and process. Analytic rubrics tend to look like checklists with multiple columns.

2. *Holistic rubrics.* The holistic rubric describes the entire process and resulting products as one interrelated event. Holistic rubrics tend to look like a paragraph with multiple outcomes.

3. *Checklists.* Rubrics can be checklists that are scored as a yes/no decision; either the learner completed the task or did not complete the

task. For example, is the student's name on the paper? This is a yes/no decision. However, if you want the full name, the name written last name first, or the name written on every page, then you have a reason for identifying levels for partial completion. Only when there is a clear-cut division between yes and no can you use a checklist.

Objectivity can be maintained with yes/no decisions. Once outcomes are scored by levels and ranges, subjectivity enters the scene. After you design your assignments and rubrics, you are strongly urged to complete each assignment, score it against the rough draft of your rubric, and decide if your rubric allows for fair and easy scoring.

Checklists also can be used to indicate what has been learned, what is being learned, and what is yet to be learned. Modeling the use of checklists with your learners equips them to become more organized and responsible both at school and in life.

4. *Chronological rubrics.* Rubrics can be completed once or revisited over time to show continuing progress. For example, when a student is memorizing the multiplication tables and being scored through oral assessments, the rubric may include a series of columns for each week's accomplishments. A chronological rubric provides a wonderful tool for everyone to keep track of the learner's progress. You can use them to record practicing spelling words at school and at home, reading aloud at school and at home, memorizing math facts, and so forth.

5. *Longitudinal rubrics.* Another kind of rubric is a longitudinal or long-range progress rubric. This rubric includes all of the criteria or outcomes included in a particular project, course of study, or grade level. As the learner demonstrates progress toward the expectation or masters the expectation, the criteria or outcome is scored. This kind of rubric is different from the chronological rubric in that the chronological rubric focuses on a single expectation over time.

6. *Process rubrics.* Process rubrics include detailed descriptors of interpersonal relationships that teachers want to instill in their students, such as cooperative learning, leadership, and so forth. Process rubrics are also used to score demonstrations, performances, outlooks, and dispositions.

7. *Product rubrics.* Product rubrics include detailed descriptors of the final product. This kind of rubric usually is a combination of analytic and holistic, in that each component of the product is specified as well as the final creation. For example, product rubrics can be used to score a research paper and presentation with visual graphics. And process and product rubrics can easily be used together.

8. *Rating scales.* A rating scale is a kind of rubric that is useful for checking students' competence, confidence, and comfort with their learning. For example, let's say you are introducing a unit about space. You can ask your students to complete a rating rubric as a pre-assessment, indicating what they know, can do, and believe regarding the unit's expectations and outcomes. With nonreaders or learners for whom English is a new language, you can use a rating scale rubric that includes pictures of faces reflecting one's understanding.

Score Your Rubrics

Here are recommendations for scoring your rubrics:

1. Select the most appropriate kind of rubric.

2. Identify the criteria for a Satisfactory score and match it to the standards and objectives. These criteria usually are placed in the middle column.

3. Write criteria in language that is academic, developmentally appropriate, and coherent.

4. Choose criteria for each level that are achievable by all learners.

5. Place criteria for exceeding a Satisfactory score in the columns to the left of center and place criteria for not meeting a Satisfactory score in the columns to the right of center.

6. Be sure that criteria in each column are consistent and parallel across columns with continuity between criteria.

7. Maintain reliability and validity when assessing your criteria.

8. Maintain salience and fairness when assessing criteria.

9. Check how all criteria are weighted.

10. Determine a clear separation between each level.

11. Add all values to see that the point allocations total the anticipated sum for the column.

12. Add all values to see that they total the anticipated sum for the rubric.

13. Incorporate all three ways of assessing (observing, listening, or reading) so the scores are conducted objectively.

14. Share the rubrics and scoring procedures with students and their families.

15. Be sure that criteria match the template.

Collaborate With Learners

As you increase your expertise with rubrics, you can begin to co-construct your rubrics with your learners. Your learners want clear guidelines and they want to participate in the process. This is the best way to give them voice, choice, and agency. Plus, here is an opportunity for you to share the work.

If most of the teachers at your school have been using rubrics with their learners, then they not only comprehend the purposes for using rubrics, they are ready to co-construct the rubrics. Start by co-constructing a rubric that will be used frequently, such as a rubric for writing or the weekly spelling activity. Leave space on the regularly used rubric for learners to customize the rubric for specific tasks. This procedure establishes entrée for the next step.

You can ask your learners for suggestions or you can let them work in cooperative learning groups to design the rubric. You could jigsaw a multi-task project by assigning a different cooperative learning group to design the rubric for each portion of the project. Co-constructing the rubric will set a positive and productive tone for learning.

Feature Self-Assessments and Peer Assessments

When it is time to assess outcomes, consider letting your learners assess their own outcome first or letting them peer assess one another's outcomes. Distributing the same rubric that you will use to assess the learners, give your learners some colored pencils. Ask the learners to make legends in the margins noting the color of pencil each learner will use to assess themselves and then to assess a peer. You could also design the rubric to include several columns for self assessment, peer assessment, and teacher assessment. Experience reveals that learners assess themselves more harshly than they assess their peers or than teachers assess them. See what happens in your classroom and what subject areas allow for self-assessment and peer assessment most effectively and efficiently.

Let Your Templates and Rubrics Do the Work for You . . .

As one teacher shared:

> *I created a template for each unit of learning and was amazed at all the ideas that flew out of my head. As I would teach one unit of*

learning, I was already thinking and planning for the next unit of learning. That's when I discovered how my curriculum was more integrated and connected; my teaching was flowing together so smoothly. My classroom became much more fun and rewarding once I stopped worrying about the scores and grades. Templates allowed me to give my students much more of my time and attention, resulting in greater achievement.

The same advice applies to rubrics. Each of these tools will serve you well.

Extend With Questions and Activities

Frequently Asked Questions About Templates

1. Should I make a performance-based assessment template for every unit of learning?

You are strongly urged to do this. You will be amazed at how quickly and easily developing the template will become for you with time and practice. You will know which assessments you use most frequently, which ones are most effective, which ones are least effective, which ones you are avoiding, and so forth. You simply cannot evaluate what you are doing until you have the data or evidence to review. Plus, and this is the bonus, once you have developed your performance-based assessments for your units of learning, you merely have to adjust them the next time. You won't believe how much planning time you will save in the future. (And your school administrators will be extremely impressed with your professionalism.)

2. What is the best way to store and access my templates?

You want to keep a copy on your computer and make a hard copy to keep with your plans. Make back-up computer copies and use technological devices that you can carry to school with you to use during your planning periods. You might want to make multiple hard copies too so you can keep an original in your files, one to check off as you complete the assessment and make notes for effectiveness, and one to record necessary future revisions. Although computers are a fantastic improvement for teachers, many thoughts will pop into your mind at times when you cannot access a computer immediately.

3. Should I share the template with my students and/or their families?

You might want to show your learners and their families your templates to illustrate how you align curriculum and instruction planned specifically for your learners. Most likely they will be quite impressed yet somewhat confused. Be sure to explain your templates carefully. It would be more effective to use your template to build the rubric for each of your performance-based assessments.

Activities for Templates

1. Select one unit of learning and fill in a template with your favorite regular activities and assignments. Now you can see your strengths and where you need to broaden your assessments.

2. Write some preassessments, formative assessments, and summative assessments in a template for a learning experience that you facilitate regularly such as your monthly good citizenship celebration.

3. Make a blank template to keep on your desk to record ideas as they occur to you throughout the day.

4. Tell a colleague about the template so the two of you can inform and support one another.

5. Identify a subject area that is more challenging for you. Ask a colleague to help you complete a template for this difficult area.

Frequently Asked Questions about Rubrics:

1. Does every lesson or learning experience need a rubric?

No. You will need to reflect upon your teaching and decide the times that rubrics are most appropriate.

2. Can I use the same rubrics repeatedly?

Yes. This is encouraged. Then your learners and their families will become accustom to the practice and can fulfill the expectations more easily. Once a comfortable routine has been established, then you can expand to a variety of rubrics.

3. How can I get families involved with rubrics?

You certainly could add a column for families to assess products too. You could select a paper or project from time-to-time and encourage the families to provide feedback. You will want to include specific directions when families participate.

Activities for Rubrics

1. Select a daily activity and write a simple rubric on your own. Ask your learners to assess themselves and to give you feedback related to the effectiveness and efficiency of the rubric.

2. Write a rubric for a unit of learning that you can use as a blueprint for future units.

3. Make a poster of your writing rubric, laminate it, and hang it on the wall for use during your writers' workshop.

4. Tell your learners how to use a rubric to improve their learning.

5. Identify one subject area for each of the six different kinds of rubrics so you can include a variety of rubrics over time.

10

Conducting Evaluation and Accountability

All of your assessments contribute to two major responsibilities of teaching: evaluation and accountability. Evaluation occurs as an overall decision that must be made after the summative assessments of a unit of learning, at the end of a grading period such as the quarter or semester, or for the entire school year. Most middle-level and secondary school students possess only an initial comprehension of the importance of grades. Students will gain more understanding and begin to realize the power of grades as they progress through school.

Accountability manifests itself as documentation of records and various lines of communication with students and their families. You are accountable for every learner every day. For some learners, you must communicate progress with families on a daily basis. You send a note or reporting form home with the student each day, checking accomplishments for the day and areas that need attention. For most of your learners, you communicate weekly, monthly, or at specific times, such as during conferences and through report forms. During conferences, you convey each learner's successes as well as his or her challenges; on report forms you must communicate the learner's progress by writing the precise message in limited space. Both evaluation and accountability are significant responsibilities that each teacher takes quite seriously and prepares for before the first day of school.

Evaluate Accomplishments

Evaluation involves making final decisions about your and your students' accomplishments. The decision-making process can be difficult as you realize the power of your pen. You determine students' grades, placements, references, and so forth. You need to be honest yet cognizant of opportunity. Examine all of the data, both quantitative and qualitative, as evidence that contributes to your decision making. Talk with seasoned colleagues and school administrators as you begin your evaluations to check your thinking. You want to know the established patterns in your school and community. Evaluation is a time to reflect upon you and your students.

Prepare to Review Outcomes

Once you have conducted your summative assessments, it is time to review outcomes. Evaluation involves analyzing and deciding the degree to which students have *mastered long-term outcomes toward learning goals.* You will evaluate all six components of assessment: the learners and learning, the teacher and teaching, the school and the schooling (see Chapter 1). You want to fully comprehend the accomplishments of your students individually and as a group, your own teaching, and the curriculum and context that you orchestrated (refer to Figure 1.1 in Chapter 1).

For example, when you teach a unit of learning on economics, you identify the goal or the big picture, such as "learning about economic decision making." The objectives of the unit address needs and wants, goods and services, resources, scarcity, choice, opportunity costs, bartering, production, work, savings, spending, and economic independence among communities, states, and nations. You design the curriculum, align your assessments, and assign instruction and activities. You create a template of assessments with all kinds of rubrics to guide the unit and outcomes. You initiate the learning, gather your assessments, and correct or redirect as needed.

Then it is time to evaluate by reviewing all of the evidence. You must decide whether each of your learners has mastered the goals and the degree or extent of their individual proficiencies. Often, your evaluation of your learners' accomplishments culminates in an over-all grade that is communicated with parents on a report form, or through parent-teacher conferences, or as passing a particular course or the entire grade level. Finally, you are responsible for the account-ability of the learning, teaching, and schooling. Evaluation and accountability operate collaboratively; one informs and supports the other as you conduct your assessments and gather the data leading to your decision making.

Establish Evaluation Criteria

Evaluation requires you to step back and see the big picture. It is easy to caught up in the everyday interactions and classroom man-agement. You want to stay focused on the learning as you conduct your assessment, collect the data, and evaluate outcomes.

Here are 10 criteria to help you evaluate outcomes:

1. Evaluation criteria are communicated with learners and families prior to being used.

2. Evaluations are conducted frequently in all stages of learning and teaching.

3. Evaluations are based on assessments that have clear and use-ful purposes.

4. Evaluations, like rubrics, are both holistic for a global overview and analytic for a diagnostic understanding of outcomes.

5. Evaluations stem from assessments that produce data and evidence documented for accountability.

6. Evaluations reflect optimal learning and teaching.

7. Evaluations include salience, validity, reliability, fidelity, and robustness.

8. Evaluations produce usable, readily interpreted scores, rat-ings, grades, and so forth.

9. Evaluations are easily read, understood, and applied to learn-ing, teaching, and schooling.

10. Evaluations can be generalized and transferred to predict future success.

Focus on Learners

The most difficult aspect of evaluation is judging your learners. You want your students to comprehend that they have earned the grade and you are not giving it to them. Learners of all ages and at all stages are challenged by this concept, and rightfully so. Too often, teachers appear to give grades without articulating purposeful activities and assignments that lead to fair assessments and anticipated evaluations with the students and their families. You want to be open, honest, and objective in your assessments and evaluations.

Judging may sound harsh, but that is exactly what you are doing as you transfer your assessments into decisions. You do not want to guess; therefore, you must maintain meticulous records all the time. Schedule an uninterrupted time every day to review your learners' accomplishments—that is, their participation, processes, and products—and make copious notes. You will not be able to remember either the general ideas or the minute details of your teaching later.

At times you want to keep copies of the evidence. In middle-level and secondary schools, students are responsible for most of their own papers. You may want to make a second copy of some of the assignments and assessments to add to the files you maintain for each of your learners. Only by reviewing the files will you be able to detect patterns of concern and create the appropriate interventions to correct and redirect learning.

As you evaluate your students, you are comparing and contrasting them against several frames of reference that you may or not realize influence your decision making. You are comparing and contrasting your students against (1) other students in the same grade or subject area, (2) other students in the same grade and subject area that you have taught in the past, (3) other students in the same grade and subject area across the state and nation, (4) what you believe students in this grade and subject area should be accomplishing, (5) the student's prior accomplishments, as well as (6) the students in this context. These six frames of references tend to be invisible, yet they control you. Although there are state curricular guidelines stipulating the student learning expectations, ultimately you are the one who judges and decides a final grade on a project or in the course. You want to be ready to defend your decisions.

Plan Your Grading Procedures

In most classrooms, evaluation and accountability conclude with grades. Check with your colleagues and school administrator before you start grading. Find out if there are particular policies and procedures at your school or within your district about grades and grading, especially about sharing grades with learners and their families.

You want to think through your grading before you ever start teaching. You want to be fully aware of your personal beliefs about grades and how your beliefs influence your behaviors. Grades must reflect your assessment and ensure validity, reliability, salience, and fairness. You might want to revisit the concepts presented in Chapter 2.

Here are 10 guidelines to use when grading. Grades should

1. Represent identified and articulated goals and objectives (see Chapter 3)

2. Match identified and articulated expectations and evidence

3. Detail each learner's individual expectations and required evidence prior to collecting formative and summative assessment data (see Chapter 3)

4. Combine formative and summative assessments from many different activities and assignments (see Chapters 4 and 5)

5. Build from learning that scaffolds, spirals, compacts, integrates, and is project based and holistic (see Chapter 5)

6. Account for learners who require additional time, resources, and assistance

7. Offer opportunities for learners to revise and resubmit assessments following interventions (Chapter 5)

8. Avoid extra-credit assessments

9. Balance participation showcasing process and product related to learning, not behavior

10. Reflect knowledge, skills, and dispositions demonstrating the learner's competence *of* learning, confidence *for* learning, and readiness *as* learning

Account for Progress

You are accountable for everything related to every student's progress as well as your own development. In addition to a planning notebook, you should set up a grade book with attendance and establish two series of files. One series of files should include a folder for each learner. These are confidential folders in which you will keep all of the correspondence and copies of correspondence that you exchange with each learner and the learner's family. You will send home daily or weekly notes with some of your learners. Your notes may be sent by U.S. mail or e-mail. If you conduct a telephone conversation, immediately make notes of who initiated the call, the date and time of the call, every time you tried to return a call, and a summary of the conversation. You may want to create a running record and attach it to the folder so you can note each correspondence, the date, and a summary of the correspondence.

You will also include notes summarizing progress in the learners' folders. Again, it is recommended that you construct a running record on which you can note the date and the event. You want to record outstanding events that are both rewarding and challenging. Include events that happen during class formally and informally, outside of class, and with other teachers.

Document and Maintain Records

The importance of documenting and maintaining records cannot be emphasized strongly enough. As you begin visualizing your curriculum, instruction, and assessments, start keeping notes for each step that you take. Try using a three-ring notebook for the first month of school with dividers for each subject area. Make three columns on your notepaper labeled Curriculum, Instruction, and Assessment. As you plan and prepare for the unit of instruction, you can streamline these three areas so you can start with curriculum, instruction, or assessment. Some teachers are more comfortable looking at standards and textbooks to guide curriculum; some teachers are more comfortable thinking about methods and activities to support instruction. However, as noted in Chapter 3, it is recommended that you begin with the end or with the outcomes and assessments so you are sure you have maximized learning.

As you collect the baseline, formative, and summative data to assess your learners and then evaluate accomplishments, you can return to your record keeping and note the effectiveness and efficiency of your plans. If you take time at the end of each school day to maintain your records, the process becomes quicker, easier, and more informative over time. You will begin to see the patterns that help you succeed and the ones that need correction and redirection.

Report Outcomes

Keeping notebooks and folders offers you the best tools for accounting for progress when you are talking with a learner, a parent, or an administrator. You will be reporting progress on weekly, monthly, or quarterly report forms. You may have to make referrals for special services, and you want to be ready. As noted in Chapter 2, assessments should be data driven; these systems help you keep the data current and complete.

You must communicate progress with the students and their parents frequently. Parents want to preview the learning before the school year even begins. During the annual open house and back-to-school night, parents will be eager to get feedback on what their children are doing, how they are behaving, and how well they are achieving. You are urged to call every learner's parent during the first two weeks of school. Many school administrators expect their teachers to do this. You want to establish a telephone protocol so you are reporting similar categories of outcomes to each parent. Parents talk with their children, and parents talk with other parents. You want to be well equipped so you are professional and consistent when talking with parents.

You could organize your conversations around the four domains (see Chapter 2) and report one positive observation related to cognitive knowledge, psychomotor skills, affective dispositions, and psychosocial interactions. Then you can add one or two questions and or concerns. Do not exceed the one- or two-item limit in any one telephone call. Then you can ask if the parents have any questions or concerns. Parents will be extremely impressed. Here is one teacher's sample call:

> *Hello, Ms. Newton, this is Mr. Thompson, Sam's calculus teacher. I wanted to call and tell you how well Sam is progressing in class. He pays close attention when new functions are introduced and completes his homework every day. He contributes positively during problem solving and gets along well with the other students. I noticed that Sam misses a few problems everyday and I think he would like to improve his scores. I am wondering how we can encourage him to proofread his work a little more carefully? Could Sam compare his work with a friend from class to see where he is overlooking the fine tuning that is necessary to improve his scores? Yes, David is in the same class. That would be a great partnership. I will suggest that they check their work with one another so they both improve their scores. Thank you for your time. Good-bye.*

You also will share progress on various report forms and in parent conferences. Your grade book with attendance records, notebooks, and folders provide the data that you will need to report progress accurately.

Concentrate on Your Effectiveness

Just as you gathered evidence to evaluate your learners, now think about the effectiveness and evidence of your own knowledge, skills, and dispositions related to the

1. Planning and preparation

2. Environment and climate

3. Instruction and activities

4. Assessments and evaluation

These four areas correspond to the four domains of Pathwise developed by Danielson (1996), now used in more than 30 states to guide teacher preparation and licensure. The four domains are detailed in Appendix B.

You want to be honest in your self-evaluation. Reflect on your efforts before, during, and after the learning and teaching. Did you do your best to

- Fulfill the state and school district standards and expectations?
- Make meaningful connections within and across the curriculum and community?
- Meet the needs and interests of each learner?
- Establish a shared learning community that was safe and inviting?
- Exude an atmosphere of care and fairness?
- Facilitate engaging and assorted learning experiences?
- Build upon learners' strengths and correct their weaknesses?
- Reinforce and reward outcomes to bolster confidence and competence?
- Model joy and satisfaction?

During your evaluation, make note of your accomplishments and celebrate your successes. However, if you are unsure of your responses to any of these questions or answered negatively to any of them, then explore avenues for assistance and professional development. If you want to be in control of your career, you can seek resources that will guide you to improve the areas that you evaluated as needing attention. Talk with a colleague or administer. Usually school districts provide an array of continuing education courses or the local university offers various courses that can fortify your teaching. There are many different resources to tap.

Understand Teachers' Practices

Teachers tend to teach the way they were taught. Most classroom teachers, especially novice teachers, acquire their practices related to curriculum, instruction, and assessment through the "apprenticeship of observation" (Lortie, 1975). Then teachers replicate the messages they have heard, the methods they have been taught, and the models they have seen that appealed to them both as K–12 grade learners and university teacher candidates. Teachers not only acknowledge and accept these patterns of learning, teacher educators and school administers depend upon these patterns of learning to guide and support novice teachers in becoming professionals. Teaching is like many other careers in our society, in that individuals are mentored into their professional fields by current practitioners.

However, the "generational perpetuation of practice" (Gallavan, 2007) may limit or misinform novice teachers about performance-based assessments. Research findings show that most teachers overly rely upon written assessments that seek primarily recognition and recall of information. Worksheets related to a particular set of pages in the textbook or questions taken from the end of the chapter comprise most assessments administered as assignments during the unit of learning. Assessments administered at the end of the units usually are written tests featuring multiple choice, true/false, and short answer questions. In many cases, worksheets, assignments, and tests are copied directly from the teacher's guide or are provided by the textbook publisher in a packet to be duplicated and distributed to learners.

Black and Wiliam (1998) called this approach a "poverty of practice." Their research reveals that teachers do not create meaningful and varied assessments; they do not administer assessments before, during, and after the instruction; and they do not administer tests to help their learners in the learning process. Assessments tend to be used almost exclusively to finalize a unit of learning and document levels of achievement.

The poverty of practice results in five significant outcomes:

1. Ineffective teaching because of teachers' overreliance on written tests

2. Ineffective learning as teachers teach to tests in ways that promote rote memorization and superficial learning

3. Negative impacts for learners who learn to do well on tests rather than learn to gain educational insights

4. Negative impacts for teachers who fail to become competent teachers

5. Misuse of data as teachers use feedback primarily for managerial control and record keeping that neglect authentic teaching and student-centered learning

Popham (2004a) also believes that teachers are experiencing assessment illiteracy. Teachers need to become better educated in their own knowledge, skills, and dispositions related to performance-based assessments as tools that measure learner progress before, during, and after the instruction. Teachers must acquire an assessment mindset by learning how to create and administer a variety of assessments that promote all kinds of learner engagement, critical thinking, and authentic expressions. Likewise, teachers must learn how to give productive feedback and modify their teaching to enhance learning. Teachers need to distinguish assessment from evaluation as two separate aspects, each with important contributions toward achievement and accountability.

Reflect On Your Practices

The evaluation and accountability processes also mean that it is time for you to reflect on the learning, teaching, and schooling. From an experienced teacher:

The quality of your outcomes depends on the quality of you and your decision-making abilities.

As a reflective practitioner (Schön, 1987), you need to step back and holistically consider the accomplishments of both your students and yourself. Three facets of reflection will help you refine your expertise:

Step 1: Provide a *technical description; narrate* the event; the interaction; your thoughts, words, and actions. Tell *what* occurred. Teachers tend to demonstrate more of a reaction (raw, edgy, and quick to speak or act) rather than a reflection during Step 1. Reactions tend to relate more to immediate information and focus more on the individuals involved in the situation.

Step 2: Provide a *contextual justification; rationalize* the description by telling more about *how* the events and interactions occurred as well as from *multiple perspectives*. Write out your own thoughts, words, and actions and the roles they played for you and others. Teachers tend to demonstrate more of a response (attentive, complete, and slower to speak or act) rather than a reaction or reflection during Step 2. Responses tend to relate more to continuing concepts and focus more on events.

Step 3: Provide a *dialectical significance; analyze* why the events and interactions occurred. Now you are writing a reflection (deliberate and mindful; much slower, more introspective, and more honest) than a reaction or a response. Reflections tend to relate more to unending understandings and focus more on ideas.

To become a well-rounded teacher, you want to evaluate your

1. Genuine care about your students and their families

2. Cultural competence across the curriculum, instruction, and assessments

3. Educational equity and fairness for all learners at all times and in all places

4. Self-efficacy in your planning, community building, facilitation, and evaluation

5. Quality reflections to improve the learning, teaching, and schooling

6. Professional development

Develop a Performance-Based Assessment Mindset . . .

At all times, you are a producer, a consumer, and a critic of performance-based assessments. Learning, teaching, and schooling unfold into a wonderful combination of artistry and science that matches your community. Throughout this text, guidance for developing performance-based assessments has equipped you to capitalize upon your imagination and capture every opportunity to make your classroom inviting, igniting, and exciting for all learners. You want to empower your learners with voice, choice, and agency for their own learning. You may spend only one school year with these young people; your mission should focus on inspiring them to find success throughout life.

As you incorporate alternative and authentic performance-based assessments throughout your school year, you will instill in your students a deep understanding for honest and valuable feedback throughout the learning and teaching. Well-aligned performance-based assessments allow your students (and you) to acquire, apply, and appreciate your curriculum and the instruction. You may not have been prepared to organize and facilitate your teaching using performance-based assessments or see them modeled by your colleagues; yet, each step you take when using them will increase everyone's success. As you develop your performance-based assessments, you positively impact the learning and become a professional agent of change. Table 10.1 presents a list to ensure your success.

Table 10.1   Developing a Performance-Based Assessment Mindset

1. Place the learner at the center.

2. Recognize that learning must be expressed in many different ways to fulfill many different expectations.

3. Seek authentic and alternative assessments as your preassessments, formative assessments, and summative assessments.

4. Co-construct assessments collaboratively with your learners, individually and as members of groups.

5. Align assessments as you both design the curriculum and context and assign the instruction and activities.

6. Offer learners multiple opportunities and many choices that build upon strengths and improve upon weaknesses.

7. Ensure that selected assessments highlight academic rigor and individual achievement.

8. Use baseline, formative, and summative data for effective evaluation and efficient accountability.

9. Create a collaborative community of learners among faculty focused on assessment and seek professional development to fortify your expertise.

10. Become a reflective practitioner.

Extend With Questions and Activities

Frequently Asked Questions

1. How can I share my assessment system with my learners' families?

You are wise to consider your assessment system(s), the ways that your learners will be evaluated, and how you will account for the progress to both the learners and their families. You want to articulate your assessment system both in writing and in person. Write a one-page paper describing your assessment system and share it with a colleague and your administrator to be sure that you are communicating clearly and completely. You can include a graphic organizer and a sample. Send the description home to families. Then, at back-to-school night, be ready to discuss the description in more detail.

2. What do I do when I change my approaches to assessment and evaluation?

In your first communications with families, be sure to state that this is the tentative plan for now and that changes will be incorporated into the systems throughout the school year. Reassure the learners and their families that when changes occur, everyone will be notified. After all, as you become an agent of change, then you, too, will change.

3. What do I do when I make mistakes?

Some mistakes will provide you with guidance, helping you to correct and redirect the learning and teaching. The mistakes probably will not be detectable to your learners and their families. However, other mistakes will be more visible, and as an advocate of change, you should be open and honest with yourself, your learners, and your learners' families about your mistakes. Once you identify the error and model how to intervene, everyone will learn right along with you. Congratulations, your impact will reach well beyond you and your classroom.

Activities

1. Select the template and favorite performance-based assessments that you constructed for your favorite unit of learning. Highlight the items that you want to incorporate as examples into your assessment system, evaluation procedures, and accountability plan.

2. Write several versions of your plans for your assessment system, evaluation, and accountability to share with learners and their families.

3. Make a chart of your systems to post in your classroom and to share with families at back-to-school night and parent conferences.

4. Tell your colleagues about your systems. Listen carefully to their feedback and recommendations.

5. Identify one aspect of your assessment systems, evaluation, and accountability that needs additional information and clarification. You may want to enroll in a graduate course at a local university or online to receive more guidance and support.

References and Readings

Airasian, P. W. (2005). *Classroom assessment: Concepts and applications* (5th ed.). Boston: McGraw-Hill.

Airasian, P. W., & Miranda, H. (2002). The role of assessment in the revised taxonomy. *Theory Into Practice, 41*(4), 249–254.

Andrade, H. (2007/2008, Dec/Jan). Self-assessment through rubrics. *Educational Leadership, 65*(4), 61–63.

Armstrong, T. (2000). *Multiple intelligences in the classroom* (2nd ed.). Alexandria, VA: Association of Supervision and Curriculum Development.

Aschblacher, P., & Alonzo, A. (2006). Examining the utility of elementary science notebooks for formative assessment purposes. *Educational Assessment, 11*(3/4), 179–203.

Bahr, D. L. (2006). Creating performance assessments in secondary math classrooms. *Mathematics in School, 35*(5), 4–8.

Bambrick-Santoyo, P. (2007/2008, Dec/Jan). Data in the driver's seat. *Educational Leadership, 65*(4), 43–46.

Bandura, A. (1989). Human agency in social cognitive theory. *American Psychologist, 44*(9), 1175–1184.

Black, P., & Wiliam, D. (1998). Assessment and classroom learning. *Assessment in education: Principles, Policy and Practice, 5*(1), 7–73.

Black, P., & Wiliam, D. (1998, Oct). Inside the black box: Raising standards through classroom assessment. *Phi Delta Kappan, 80*(2), 139–148.

Bloom, B. S. (1956). *Taxonomy of educational objectives, Handbook I: The cognitive domain.* New York: David McKay.

Bond, L. A. (1992, Sept). *Developing SCANS assessment measures: Issues and options.* Iowa City, IA: American College Testing Program, and Washington, DC: Council of Chief State School Officers.

Brookhart, S. M. (2007/2008, Dec/Jan). Feedback that fits. *Educational Leadership, 65*(4), 54–59.

Brooks, J. G., & Brooks, M. G. (1993). *In search of understanding: The case for constructivist classrooms.* Alexandria, VA: Association for Supervision and Curriculum Development.

Brown-Chidsey, R. (2007). No more "waiting to fail." *Educational Leadership, 65*(2), 40–46.

Bruner, J. (1966). *Studies in cognitive growth: A collaboration at the Center for Cognitive Studies.* New York: Wiley.

Bruner, J. (2004). *Toward a theory of instruction* (new ed.). Cambridge, MA: Harvard University Press.

Butlerman-Bos, J., Terwel, J., Verloop, N., & Wardekker, W. (2002). Observation in teaching: Toward a practice of objectivity. *Teachers College Record, 104*(6), 1069–1100.

Campbell, C., & Evans, J. A. (2000). Investigation of preservice teachers' classroom assessment practices during student teaching. *Journal of Educational Research, 93*(6), 350–356.

Cooper, J. D. (1997). *Literacy: Helping children construct meaning* (3rd ed., pp. 516–518). Boston: Houghton Mifflin.

Christensen, L. (2004–2005). Moving beyond judgment. *Rethinking Schools, 19*(2), 33–37.

Costa, A., & Kallick, B. (2004). *Assessment strategies for self-directed learning.* Thousand Oaks, CA: Corwin Press.

Csikszentmihalyi, M. (1997). *Creativity: Flow and the psychology of discovery and invention.* London: Harper Perennial.

Daggett, W. R. (2005, Sept). *Achieving academic excellence through rigor and relevance.* International Center for Leadership Education. Retrieved January 10, 2008, from http://www.leadered.com/pdf/Academic_Excellence.pdf

Danielson, C. (1996). *Enhancing professional practice: A framework for teaching* (2nd ed.). Alexandria, VA: Association for Supervision and Curriculum Development.

Dettmer, P. (2006). New blooms in established fields: Four domains of learning and doing. *Roeper Review, 28*(2), 70–8.

Dewey, J. (1933). *How we think.* Boston: D. C. Heath.

Dewey, J. (1997). *Experience and education.* New York: MacMillan.

DiMartino, J. (2007, Apr 25). Accountability or mastery? *Education Week, 26*(34), 44, 36.

Earl, L. (2003). *Assessment as learning: Using classroom assessment to maximize student learning.* Thousand Oaks, CA: Corwin Press.

Eisner, E. W. (1999, May). The uses and limits of performance assessment. *Phi Delta Kappan, 80*(9), 658–660.

Erickson, E. (1950). *Childhood and society.* New York: Norton.

Falk, B. (1998). Testing the way children learn: Principles for valid literacy assessments. *Language Arts, 76*(1), 57–66.

Feuerstein, R., Klein, P. S., & Tannenbaum, A. J. (1991). *Mediate learning experiences: Theoretical, psychosocial, and learning implications.* London: Freund.

Fisher, D., & Frey, N. (2007). *Checking for understanding: Formative assessment techniques for your classroom.* Alexandria, VA: Association for Supervision and Curriculum Development.

Gallavan, N. P. (2007). Seven perceptions that influence novice teachers' efficacy and cultural competence. *Praxis: The Center for Multicultural Education, 2*(1), 2–22.

Gardner, H. (1993). *Frames of mind: The theory of multiple intelligences* (10th ed.). New York: Basic Books.

Gardner, H. (2006). *Multiple intelligences: New horizons.* New York: Basic Books.

Garner, B. K. (2007). *Getting to got it.* Alexandria, VA: Association of Supervision and Curriculum Development.

Goodwin, A. L. (Ed.). (1999). *Assessment for equity and inclusion: Embracing all our children.* New York: Routledge.

Grisham-Brown, J., Hallam, R., & Brookshire, R. (2006). Using authentic assessment to evidence children's progress towards early learning standards. *Early Childhood Education Journal, 34*(1), 45–51.

Guskey, T. R. (2007/2008, Dec/Jan). The rest of the story. *Educational Leadership, 65*(4), 28–35.

Harrow, A. (1972). *A taxonomy of psychomotor domain: A guide for developing behavior objects.* New York: David McKay.

Hattie, J., & Timperley, H. (2007). The power of feedback. *Review of Educational Research, 77*(1), 81–112.

Heafner, T. (2004, Winter). Assessment as a magnification, internal, parallel, and external reflection. *Action in Teacher Education, 25*(4), 14–19.

Herman, J. L., Aschbacher, P. R., & Winters, L. (1992). *A practical guide to alternative assessment.* Alexandria, VA: Association for Supervision and Curriculum Development.

Holzberg, C. S. (2005). Designing rubrics. *Technology & Learning, 26*(3), 36, 38.

Inman, L., & Tollefson, N. (2006). Elementary teachers' attitudes towards preassessment procedures. *Psychology in the Schools, 25*(3), 331–337.

Jensen, E. (2005). *Teaching with the brain in mind* (2nd ed.). Alexandria, VA: Association for Supervision and Curriculum Development.

Jensen, M. (2006). *Mindladder: Dynamic assessment and classroom learning.* Roswell, GA: International Center for Mediated Learning.

Johnson, M. H. (2000, Spring). A district-wide agenda to improve teaching and learning in mathematics. *Journal of Classroom Interaction, 35*(1), 1–7.

Johnston, P., & Costello, P. (2005). Principles for literacy assessment. *Reading Research Quarterly, 40*(2), 256–267.

Jones, J., & Courtney, R. (2002). Documenting early science learning. *Young Children, 57*(5), 34–40.

Kiker, J. (2007). Move beyond "seat-time" and narrowly defined knowledge and skills. *Techniques (Association for Career and Technical Education), 82*(5), 38–40.

King, P. E., & Behnke, R. R. (2005, Spring). Problems associated with evaluating student performance in groups. *College Teaching, 53*(2), 57–61.

Kohlberg, L. (1958). *The development of modes of moral thinking and choice in the years 10 to 16.* Unpublished doctoral dissertation, University of Chicago.

Kohlberg, L. (1984). *The psychology of moral development. Essays on moral development* (Vol. 2). San Francisco: Harper & Row.

Kohn, A. (1999). *The schools our children deserve: Moving beyond traditional classrooms and tougher standards.* Boston: Houghton Mifflin.

Kohn, A. (2001, Jan). Fighting the tests: A practical guide to rescuing our schools. *Phi Delta Kappan, 82*(5), 348–357.

Krathwohl, D. R., Bloom, B. S., & Masia, B. B. (1964). *Taxonomy of educational objectives: Handbook II: Affective domain.* New York: David McKay.

Ladson-Billings, G. (1995). But that's just good teaching! The case for culturally relevant pedagogy. *Theory Into Practice, 34*(3), 159–165.

Lane, S., Parke, C. S., & Stone, C. A. (2002). The impact of a state performance-based assessment and accountability program on mathematics: Evidence from survey data and school performance. *Educational Assessment, 8*(4), 279–315.

Lenski, S. D., Ehlers-Zavala, F., & Daniel, M. C. (2006). Assessment English-language learners in mainstream classrooms. *Educational Assessment, 8*(4), 24–34.

Lortie, D. C. (1975). *Schoolteacher: A sociological study.* Chicago: University of Chicago Press.

Lukin, L. E., Bandolas, D. L., Eckhout, T. J., & Mickelson, K. (2004, June). Facilitating the development of assessment literacy. *Educational Measurement: Issues and Practice, 23,* 26–32.

Lund, J. L., & Kirk, M. F. (2002). *Performance-based assessment for middle and high school physical education.* Champaign, IL : Human Kinetics.

Margolis, J. (2006). New teachers, high-stakes diversity, and the performance-based conundrum. *Urban Review, 38*(1), 27–44.

Marzano, R. J. (2000). *Designing a new taxonomy of educational objectives.* Thousand Oaks, CA: Corwin Press.

Marzano, R. J., Pickering, D. J., & Pollock, J. E. (2001). *Classroom instruction that works: Research-based strategies for increasing student achievement.* Alexandria, VA: Association for Supervision and Curriculum Development.

Maslovaty, N., & Kuxi, E. (2002). Promoting motivational goals through alternative or traditional assessment. *Studies in Educational Evaluation, 28*(3), 199–222.

Maslow, A. (1943). Theory of human motivation. *Psychological Review, 50,* 370–396.

McNair, S., Bhargava, A., & Adams, L. (2003, Fall). Teachers speak out on assessment practices. *Early Childhood Education Journal, 31*(1), 23–31.

McTighe, J., & O'Connor, K. (2005). Seven practices for effective learning. *Educational Leadership, 63*(3), 10–17.

Mertler, C. A. (2001). *Classroom assessment: A practical guide for educators.* Los Angeles: Pyrczak Publishing.

Moskal, B. M. (2003). Recommendations for developing classroom performance assessments and scoring rubrics. *Practical Assessment, Research & Evaluation, 8*(14). Retrieved January 20, 2008, from http://pareonline.net/getvn.asp?v=8&n=14

O'Malley, J. M., & Valdez Pierce, L. (1996). *Authentic assessment for English language learners: Practical approaches for teachers.* Reading, MA: Addison-Wesley.

Oz, K. (2002). *Where does performance-based assessment fit in with the high stakes test environment, especially for English language learners?* Retrieved January 10, 2008, from http://www.englishhorizons.com/articles/perfbasedassessmentinlearningenglish.asp

Palincsar, A. S., & Brown, A. (1984). Reciprocal teaching of comprehension-fostering and comprehension-monitoring activities. *Cognition and Instruction, 1*(2), 117–175.

Palincsar, A. S., & Brown, A. (1986). Interactive teaching to promote independent learning from text. *The Reading Teacher, 39*(8), 771–777.

Piaget, J. (1952). *The origins of intelligence in children.* New York: Norton.

Piaget, J. (1990). *The child's conception of the world.* New York: Littlefield Adams.

Popham, W. J. (2004a). *Classroom assessment: What teachers need to know* (4th ed.). Boston: Allyn & Bacon.

Popham, W. J. (2004b). Why assessment illiteracy is professional suicide. *Educational Leadership, 62*(1), 82–83.

Popham, W. J. (2006). Phony formative assessments: Buyer beware! *Educational Leadership, 64*(3), 86–87.

Posner, D. (2004). What's wrong with teaching to the test? *Phi Delta Kappan, 85*(10), 749–751.

Postholm, M. B. (2006). Assessment during project work. *Teaching and Teacher Education, 22*(2), 150–163.

Power, B. M. (1999). Take note! *Creative Classroom, 15*(3), 50–53.

Priesz, P. A. (2006, May/June). Leaders for high school reform. *Leadership, 35*(5), 8–10.

Restak, R. (2003). *The new brain: How the modern age is rewiring your mind.* New York: Rodale.

Sadker, M., & Sadker, D. (1994). *Failing at fairness: How America's schools cheat girls.* New York: Simon & Schuster.

Schappe, J. F. (2005). Early childhood assessment: A correlational study of the relationships among student performance, student feelings, and teacher perceptions. *Early Childhood Education Journal, 33*(3), 187–193.

Schön, D. A. (1987). *Educating the reflective practitioner: Toward a design for teaching and learning in the professions.* San Francisco: Jossey-Bass.

Shepard, L. A. (2005). Linking formative assessment to scaffolding. *Educational Leadership, 63*(3), 66–70.

Shepard, L. A. (2007). Formative assessment: Caveat emptor. In C. A. Dyer (Ed.), *The future of assessment: Shaping teaching and learning* (pp. 279–303). Mahwah, NJ: Erlbaum.

Shulman, L. S. (2007). Knowledge and teaching: Foundations of the new reform. *Harvard Educational Review, 57*(1), 1–22.

Sikes, E., & Sterling, D. R. (2006). Assessment with pumpkins. *Science Scope, 30*(2), 25–26.

Simpson, E. J. (1972). *The classification of educational objectives in the psychomotor domain.* Washington, DC: Gryphon House.

Smith, L. M. (2006). The conception of reflective practice. *Perspectives in Education, 22*(2), 72–90.

Smyth, T. S. (2005). Respect, reciprocity, and reflection in the classroom. *Kappa Delta Pi Record, 42*(1), 38–41.

Starkman, N. (2006). Building a better student. *T. H. E. Journal, 33*(14), 40–42.

Sternberg, R. J. (2003). *Wisdom, intelligence, and creativity synthesized.* New York: Cambridge University Press.

Stiggins, R. (2007). Assessment through the students' eyes. *Educational Leadership, 64*(8), 22–26.

Stiggins, R. (2008). *An introduction to student-involved classroom assessment* (5th ed.). Upper Saddle River, NJ: Prentice Hall.

Taggart, G. L., Phifer, S. J., Nixon, J. A., & Wood, M. (Eds.). (1998). *Rubrics: A handbook for construction and use.* Lanham, MD: Scarecrow Education.

Templeton, R. A. (2004, July/Aug). Communication in assessing student learning: A critique of assessment tasks used in middle school science. *Clearing House, 77*(6), 253–259.

Tomlinson, C. A. (2007/2008, Dec/Jan). Learning to love assessment. *Educational Leadership, 65*(4), 8–13.

Tomlinson, C. A., & McTighe, J. (2006). *Integrating differential instruction and understanding by design: Connecting content and kids.* Alexandria, VA: Association for Supervision and Curriculum Development.

VanDeWeghe, R. (2007). How does assessment affect creativity? *English Journal, 96*(5), 91–93.

Van Manan, M. (1977). Linking ways of knowing with ways of being practical. *Curriculum Inquiry, 6*(3), 205–228.

Vygotsky, L. (1986). *Thought and language.* Boston: MIT Press.

Vygotsky, L. S. (1980). *Mind in society: The development of higher psychological processes* (M. Cole, V. John-Steiner, S. Scribner, E. Souberman, Eds. & Trans.). Cambridge, MA: Harvard University Press. (Original work published 1934)

Wiggins, G., & McTighe, J. (1998). *Understanding by design.* Alexandria, VA: Association for Supervision and Curriculum Development.

Wiliam, D. (2007/2008, Dec/Jan). Changing classroom practice. *Educational Leadership, 65*(4), 36–42.

Wink, J. (2004). *Critical pedagogy: Notes from the real world* (3rd ed.). Boston: Allyn & Bacon.

Wolfe, P. (2001). *Brain matters: Translating research into classroom practice.* Alexandria, VA: Association for Supervision and Curriculum Development.

Zeichner, K. M. (1987). Preparing reflective teachers: An overview of instructional strategies which have been employed in preservice teacher education. *International Journal of Educational Research, 11*(5), 565–576.

Zeichner, K. M., & Liston, D. P. (1987). Teaching student teachers to reflect. *Harvard Educational Review, 57,* 23–48.

Index

CORWIN PRESS

The Corwin Press logo—a raven striding across an open book—represents the union of courage and learning. Corwin Press is committed to improving education for all learners by publishing books and other professional development resources for those serving the field of PreK–12 education. By providing practical, hands-on materials, Corwin Press continues to carry out the promise of its motto: **"Helping Educators Do Their Work Better."**